HEALTH CARE IN TRANSITION

PRIVATE HEALTH INSURANCE AND THE AFFORDABLE CARE ACT

PROVISIONS AND REFORMS

HEALTH CARE IN TRANSITION

Additional books in this series can be found on Nova's website under the Series tab.

Additional E-books in this series can be found on Nova's website under the E-book tab.

HEALTH CARE IN TRANSITION

PRIVATE HEALTH INSURANCE AND THE AFFORDABLE CARE ACT

PROVISIONS AND REFORMS

DUKE RIGGS

EDITOR

NOVINKA

New York

For permission to use material from this book please contact us:
Telephone 631-231-7269; Fax 631-231-8175
Web Site: http://www.novapublishers.com

Additional color graphics may be available in the e-book version of this book.

Library of Congress Cataloging-in-Publication Data

ISBN: 978-1-62948-770-0

Published by Nova Science Publishers, Inc. † New York

CONTENTS

Preface		**vii**
Chapter 1	Overview of Private Health Insurance Provisions in the Patient Protection and Affordable Care Act (ACA) *Annie L. Mach*	**1**
Chapter 2	Private Health Plans Under the ACA: In Brief *Bernadette Fernandez and Annie L. Mach*	**37**
Chapter 3	Private Health Insurance Market Reforms in the Patient Protection and Affordable Care Act (ACA) *Annie L. Mach and Bernadette Fernandez*	**53**
Chapter 4	The Affordable Care Act and Small Business: Economic Issues *Sean Lowry and Jane G. Gravelle*	**83**
Index		**115**

PREFACE

Private health insurance (PHI) is the predominate form of health insurance coverage in the United States. The Patient Protection and Affordable Care Act, as amended, expands federal private health insurance market requirements, and requires the creation of health insurance exchanges (marketplaces) to provide certain individuals and small employers access to private insurance, among other provisions. This book explains in further detail these private health insurance market reforms in the ACA and discusses the economic issues of the ACA.

Chapter 1 - Private health insurance (PHI) is the predominate form of health insurance coverage in the United States, covering about two-thirds of Americans in 2011. The Patient Protection and Affordable Care Act (ACA, P.L. 111-148, as amended) includes provisions that restructure the private health insurance market by (1) implementing market reforms that impose requirements on private health insurance plans and sponsors of health insurance (e.g., employers); (2) creating marketplaces, "exchanges," where individuals can shop for and purchase health plans that meet or exceed federal standards; (3) providing financial assistance to qualified individuals who purchase health plans through an exchange; (4) establishing an individual mandate that requires most individuals to either maintain health insurance coverage or pay a penalty; and (5) assessing penalties on certain employers that either do not provide health insurance or provide health insurance that is "unaffordable" or does not provide "minimum value."

The ACA provisions build on and modify the existing structure of the PHI market. In the PHI market, most individuals receive coverage through the group market (i.e., from an employer or association). Prior to the passage of ACA, the group market had many protections for individuals, such as limiting pre-existing condition exclusions and prohibiting discrimination based on health status. However, access to coverage in the group market could be different depending on the size of the group. In general, the size and composition of a group can affect both an organization's decision to offer coverage and the cost of that coverage to an enrollee. As a result, smaller groups are less likely to offer coverage than larger groups, and members of smaller groups are less likely to enroll in the coverage than members of larger groups. Some individuals purchase nongroup, or individual, coverage in the PHI market. Prior to the passage of ACA, nongroup coverage typically provided fewer protections than group coverage. For example, subject to state law, insurers offering coverage in the nongroup market could deny coverage to applicants who had pre-existing conditions or a history of health problems.

The PHI market reform provisions in ACA affect health insurance offered to groups and individuals, impose requirements on sponsors of coverage, and, collectively, establish minimum requirements with respect to access to coverage, premiums, benefits, cost-sharing, and consumer protections. Some market reforms are already in effect, such as the requirement for certain health plans to provide dependent coverage up to age 26. Beginning in 2014, when more of the market reforms take effect, certain health plans will have to offer a somewhat standardized set of benefits, called the essential health benefits (EHB), and certain health plans will have to accept all individuals who apply for coverage, regardless of health status and pre-existing conditions.

ACA's new marketplaces, the exchanges, must be operational in every state in time for the first exchange open season, which begins October 1, 2013. Coverage under exchange plans will begin as early as January 1, 2014. In addition to individuals shopping for and obtaining nongroup health insurance coverage through exchanges, some individuals may be eligible to receive financial assistance for the cost of that coverage in the form of premium tax credits and cost-sharing subsidies. Small employers will be able to purchase coverage to offer to their employees through small business health options program (SHOP) exchanges; however, ACA limits the SHOPs to small employers with either 50 or fewer employees or 100 or fewer employees, at state option.

Another ACA requirement is that most individuals must either maintain health insurance coverage or pay a penalty. The "individual mandate" goes into effect in 2014. To comply with the mandate, most individuals will have to maintain "minimum essential coverage," which includes coverage obtained through exchanges, employer-sponsored insurance, nongroup coverage, and coverage from a federal program such as Medicare and Medicaid. Certain individuals are exempt from the individual mandate penalty, such as those with qualifying religious exemptions and those whose household income is less than the filing threshold for federal income taxes for the applicable tax year.

Employers play an important role in providing coverage in the existing PHI market, and ACA includes two provisions that could influence an employer's decision to offer health benefits. First, certain small employers may be eligible to receive tax credits. To be eligible, small employers cannot have more than 25 full-time equivalent employees and must contribute a uniform percentage of at least 50% to their employees' health insurance coverage. The tax credit became available in 2010, and it is available for a total of six years. Second, beginning in 2014, ACA imposes penalties on employers with at least 50 full-time equivalent employees, if one or more of their full-time employees obtain a premium tax credit through an exchange. Individuals who meet certain requirements may be eligible for a premium tax credit if their employer does not offer health insurance coverage, or if their employer offers coverage that is "unaffordable" or does not provide "minimum value," as defined by ACA.

This report provides an overview of ACA provisions that affect the PHI market. In general, the ACA provisions build on or modify the existing structure of the PHI market, and a short background on the existing structure is included in the report. While this report provides a broad overview of the PHI provisions in ACA, the reader may be interested in more in-depth discussions on specific aspects of the law.

The Patient Protection and Affordable Care Act (ACA, P.L. 111-148, as amended) includes a number of provisions that affect the private health insurance market. The provisions create new rules and incentives for entities and individuals in the market that build on and modify the existing market structure. Collectively, the provisions reflect a general goal of ACA to increase access to health insurance coverage.

The provisions have been gradually implemented since ACA was enacted (in 2010). In 2014 when most will be effective, nearly all individuals will be able to obtain private coverage regardless of pre-existing conditions or health status, and insurers will have limited ability to vary premiums based on an applicant's health status and other characteristics. To help accommodate individuals who will have access to private health insurance as a result of these (and other) provisions, individuals and small businesses will be able to shop for and purchase private coverage in new marketplaces, "exchanges."

Additionally, some individuals will receive financial assistance toward coverage obtained in an exchange.

The market reform provisions attempt to increase access to private coverage for many individuals, including those who are sick. ACA also includes a "shared responsibility" requirement, which does not allow healthy individuals to wait to buy coverage until it is needed without incurring a penalty for doing so. Many argued that unless healthy individuals were encouraged to participate in the private market, insurance pools would become overrun with individuals who are high users of health care services, potentially creating financially unstable situations for insurers and enrollees. Beginning in 2014, most individuals will be required to maintain health insurance coverage or otherwise pay a penalty, and employers will have new financial incentives to consider when determining whether to offer employer-based health insurance to employees.

This report begins with a short background on the existing structure of the private health insurance market. It is important to understand the features of the existing market as a way to understand public policies, such as ACA, that affect the market. Descriptions of ACA provisions follow; each provision is considered within the context of the existing structure of the market.

Chapter 2 - The Patient Protection and Affordable Care Act (ACA, P.L. 111-148), as amended, expands federal private health insurance market requirements, and requires the creation of health insurance exchanges (marketplaces) to provide certain individuals and small employers access to private insurance, among other provisions. While some of ACA's private insurance provisions have already become effective, full implementation begins in 2014 and beyond. Given the breadth of ACA's reforms to the existing private insurance market and creation of new health insurance marketplaces, there is interest in understanding what types of health plans may be offered once these ACA provisions are fully implemented.

This report provides short descriptions of health plans that may be offered inside and outside of exchanges, and includes information about interaction with other selected ACA provisions. The descriptions are displayed in a side-by-side format to facilitate comparison of exchange and non-exchange plans. This report does not attempt to identify all forms of health insurance coverage, but does address all plan types specified under ACA's exchange provisions, as well as major medical plans and certain limited benefit plans offered outside of exchanges. In addition, this report indicates the applicability of ACA's market reforms to plans offered in the private market.

Chapter 3 - The private health insurance provisions in the Patient Protection and Affordable Care Act (ACA, P.L. 111-148, as amended) include market reforms that impose requirements on private health insurance plans. Such reforms relate to the offer, issuance, generosity, and pricing of health plans, among other requirements.

ACA's market reforms largely focus on the individual and small group health insurance markets, and in this report the reforms have been grouped by effective dates: "immediate" market reforms that become effective *prior* to the full implementation date of ACA, and reforms that become effective *on* the full implementation date (January 1, 2014).

ACA requires implementation of a number of reforms prior to its full implementation date (i.e., prior to plan years beginning on or after January 1, 2014). "Immediate" reforms include a process to review unreasonable rate increases; an Internet portal to assist consumers in identifying coverage options; prohibition on lifetime limits and restriction of annual limits; the prohibition on rescissions; coverage of preventive health services with no cost-sharing; extension of dependent coverage; prohibition of discrimination based on salary; standards related to medical loss ratios and rebates to plan participants; appeals processes; coverage of preexisting health conditions for children; patient protections; uniform explanation of coverage documents; and reporting requirements regarding quality of care.

Market reforms effective beginning in 2014 include nondiscrimination based on health status; guaranteed issue and guaranteed renewability; coverage of preexisting health conditions (regardless of age); nondiscrimination regarding clinical trial participation; rating restrictions; waiting period limitation; and nondiscrimination regarding health care providers.

This report provides background information about the private health insurance market, including market segments and regulation. It describes each ACA market reform and notes any major implementation activity that has occurred (e.g., issuance of final rule from a department such as Health and Human Services). The appendices of the report provide additional information about the status of regulations relating to each reform and how the reforms apply to the different market segments and health plans.

Chapter 4 - The Patient Protection and Affordable Care Act (ACA; P.L. 111-148 and P.L. 111-152) contains several provisions to encourage employer-sponsored health coverage, particularly among small businesses. The provisions that most directly relate to small businesses are (1) an employer penalty for not providing health insurance, (2) a tax credit to increase the affordability of health care for the smallest firms, and (3) small business health insurance exchanges designed to increase plan options and lower plan costs.

Several events have altered ACA's implementation since its enactment in 2010. Most notably, the Obama administration delayed the implementation of the employer penalty and part of the small business health exchanges from 2014 to 2015 to allow for more time for developing these provisions and allowing firms to come into compliance. These delays have added to uncertainty over the potential effects of ACA on small businesses.

First, this report explains how employer-sponsored insurance can be used to address concerns about health insurance coverage and cost. Second, it summarizes the three ACA provisions most relevant to small businesses, listed above. Next, it analyzes these provisions for their potential effects on small businesses. Last, this report presents several approaches that could address some concerns associated with these provisions (particularly the employer penalty).

According to analysis of the most recent employer size and insurance coverage data, ACA's employer penalty is structured so that it could exempt approximately 96.3% of employer firms simply because they would be too small, and thus fall below the employer penalty threshold of 50 full-time equivalent (FTE) employees. These exempt firms account for approximately 28.1% of all workers. After accounting for firms that already provide insurance, less than 1% of employer firms could be subject to the employer penalty. Although 71.9% of all employees work for firms that are large enough to be potentially subject to the penalty, only about 1.7% of employees work in firms that do not already offer health insurance.

Less than 4% of small businesses that could have been eligible for the small business health care tax credit in 2010 actually claimed it. According to a report by the Government Accountability Office (GAO), many business owners felt that (1) the credit was too small of an incentive to begin offering insurance; (2) even if these small employers offered health insurance, some employees declined coverage because they felt that they cannot afford their share of the premium; and (3) the rules were too complex. President Obama has proposed simplifying and expanding the credit.

Small business health exchanges could help to reduce some barriers to accessing relatively affordable health coverage in the small-group market. By pooling risk among multiple businesses and reducing administrative costs, average insurance costs could reduce costs for these firms. On the other hand, firms with relatively healthier employees could see a rise in insurance costs.

In: Private Health Insurance … ISBN: 978-1-62948-770-0
Editor: Duke Riggs

Chapter 1

OVERVIEW OF PRIVATE HEALTH INSURANCE PROVISIONS IN THE PATIENT PROTECTION AND AFFORDABLE CARE ACT (ACA)*

Annie L. Mach

SUMMARY

Private health insurance (PHI) is the predominate form of health insurance coverage in the United States, covering about two-thirds of Americans in 2011. The Patient Protection and Affordable Care Act (ACA, P.L. 111-148, as amended) includes provisions that restructure the private health insurance market by (1) implementing market reforms that impose requirements on private health insurance plans and sponsors of health insurance (e.g., employers); (2) creating marketplaces, "exchanges," where individuals can shop for and purchase health plans that meet or exceed federal standards; (3) providing financial assistance to qualified individuals who purchase health plans through an exchange; (4) establishing an individual mandate that requires most individuals to either maintain health insurance coverage or pay a penalty; and (5) assessing penalties on certain employers that either do not

* This is an edited, reformatted and augmented version of a Congressional Research Service publication, CRS Report for Congress R43048, dated April 23, 2013.

provide health insurance or provide health insurance that is "unaffordable" or does not provide "minimum value."

The ACA provisions build on and modify the existing structure of the PHI market. In the PHI market, most individuals receive coverage through the group market (i.e., from an employer or association). Prior to the passage of ACA, the group market had many protections for individuals, such as limiting pre-existing condition exclusions and prohibiting discrimination based on health status. However, access to coverage in the group market could be different depending on the size of the group. In general, the size and composition of a group can affect both an organization's decision to offer coverage and the cost of that coverage to an enrollee. As a result, smaller groups are less likely to offer coverage than larger groups, and members of smaller groups are less likely to enroll in the coverage than members of larger groups. Some individuals purchase nongroup, or individual, coverage in the PHI market. Prior to the passage of ACA, nongroup coverage typically provided fewer protections than group coverage. For example, subject to state law, insurers offering coverage in the nongroup market could deny coverage to applicants who had pre-existing conditions or a history of health problems.

The PHI market reform provisions in ACA affect health insurance offered to groups and individuals, impose requirements on sponsors of coverage, and, collectively, establish minimum requirements with respect to access to coverage, premiums, benefits, cost-sharing, and consumer protections. Some market reforms are already in effect, such as the requirement for certain health plans to provide dependent coverage up to age 26. Beginning in 2014, when more of the market reforms take effect, certain health plans will have to offer a somewhat standardized set of benefits, called the essential health benefits (EHB), and certain health plans will have to accept all individuals who apply for coverage, regardless of health status and pre-existing conditions.

ACA's new marketplaces, the exchanges, must be operational in every state in time for the first exchange open season, which begins October 1, 2013. Coverage under exchange plans will begin as early as January 1, 2014. In addition to individuals shopping for and obtaining nongroup health insurance coverage through exchanges, some individuals may be eligible to receive financial assistance for the cost of that coverage in the form of premium tax credits and cost-sharing subsidies. Small employers will be able to purchase coverage to offer to their employees through small business health options program (SHOP) exchanges; however, ACA limits the SHOPs to small employers with either 50 or fewer employees or 100 or fewer employees, at state option.

Another ACA requirement is that most individuals must either maintain health insurance coverage or pay a penalty. The "individual mandate" goes into effect in 2014. To comply with the mandate, most individuals will have to maintain "minimum essential coverage," which includes coverage obtained through exchanges, employer-sponsored insurance, nongroup coverage, and coverage from a federal program such as Medicare and Medicaid. Certain individuals are exempt from the individual mandate penalty, such as those with qualifying religious exemptions and those whose household income is less than the filing threshold for federal income taxes for the applicable tax year.

Employers play an important role in providing coverage in the existing PHI market, and ACA includes two provisions that could influence an employer's decision to offer health benefits. First, certain small employers may be eligible to receive tax credits. To be eligible, small employers cannot have more than 25 full-time equivalent employees and must contribute a uniform percentage of at least 50% to their employees' health insurance coverage. The tax credit became available in 2010, and it is available for a total of six years. Second, beginning in 2014, ACA imposes penalties on employers with at least 50 full-time equivalent employees, if one or more of their full-time employees obtain a premium tax credit through an exchange. Individuals who meet certain requirements may be eligible for a premium tax credit if their employer does not offer health insurance coverage, or if their employer offers coverage that is "unaffordable" or does not provide "minimum value," as defined by ACA.

This report provides an overview of ACA provisions that affect the PHI market. In general, the ACA provisions build on or modify the existing structure of the PHI market, and a short background on the existing structure is included in the report. While this report provides a broad overview of the PHI provisions in ACA, the reader may be interested in more in-depth discussions on specific aspects of the law.

The Patient Protection and Affordable Care Act (ACA, P.L. 111-148, as amended) includes a number of provisions that affect the private health insurance market. The provisions create new rules and incentives for entities and individuals in the market that build on and modify the existing market structure. Collectively, the provisions reflect a general goal of ACA to increase access to health insurance coverage.

The provisions have been gradually implemented since ACA was enacted (in 2010). In 2014 when most will be effective, nearly all individuals will be able to obtain private coverage regardless of pre-existing conditions or health status, and insurers will have limited ability to vary premiums based on an applicant's health status and other characteristics. To help accommodate individuals who will have access to private health insurance as a result of these (and other) provisions, individuals and small businesses will be able to shop for and purchase private coverage in new marketplaces, "exchanges." Additionally, some individuals will receive financial assistance toward coverage obtained in an exchange.

The market reform provisions attempt to increase access to private coverage for many individuals, including those who are sick. ACA also includes a "shared responsibility" requirement, which does not allow healthy individuals to wait to buy coverage until it is needed without incurring a penalty for doing so. Many argued that unless healthy individuals were encouraged to participate in the private market, insurance pools would become overrun with individuals who are high users of health care services, potentially creating financially unstable situations for insurers and enrollees.[1] Beginning in 2014, most individuals will be required to maintain health insurance coverage or otherwise pay a penalty, and employers will have new financial incentives to consider when determining whether to offer employer-based health insurance to employees.

This report begins with a short background on the existing structure of the private health insurance market. It is important to understand the features of the existing market as a way to understand public policies, such as ACA, that affect the market. Descriptions of ACA provisions follow; each provision is considered within the context of the existing structure of the market.[2]

BACKGROUND

Americans obtain health insurance coverage in different settings and through a variety of methods. While many receive coverage through publicly funded programs, such as Medicare and Medicaid, private health insurance is the predominate form of health coverage in the United States. In 2011, 65% of the population had private health insurance. Most individuals and families obtain private insurance through group coverage, such as employer-sponsored insurance (ESI); about 57% of the population had ESI in 2011. Some individuals and families may purchase private insurance on their own in the nongroup, or individual, market. Approximately 12% of the population had nongroup coverage in 2011.[3]

The private health insurance market in the United States is sometimes described as "patchwork." The patchwork nature of the market is reflected, in part, in that often an individual's ability to obtain and maintain comprehensive private coverage is different in each of the three market segments: large group, small group, and nongroup.[4] Additionally, access to comprehensive and affordable private insurance can be affected by factors such as state residency, health status, and employment status. Understanding the patchwork nature of the private market helps explain why not all individuals have the same opportunities, experiences, and outcomes in the market. For example, some types of private firms are more likely to offer group coverage to their employees (e.g., private firms that consider at least three-quarters of their workers "full-time"), and as follows, individuals who work at these firms (at least those who are full-time) may have more access to private coverage compared to individuals who work at firms that do not offer coverage.

Individuals who have group coverage typically obtain this coverage as part of a compensation package received through his/her own employment or a family member's employment. Health insurance coverage provided by larger employers or associations has several attributes. The coverage is usually comprehensive and subsidized by the sponsor of the group plan (e.g., the employer). An individual's access to this coverage depends on access to the group, but it does not typically depend on the individual's health status or demographic characteristics, such as age.

Table 1. Percentage of Private Sector Firms that Offer Health Insurance, by Firm Size, 2011

Firm Size	Number of Firms	Percent That Offer Health Insurance
Less than 10 employees	3,809,084	28.3%
10-24 employees	748,434	58.4%
25-99 employees	510,114	78.1%
100-999 employees	452,731	93.3%
1000 or more employees	991,162	99.5%

Source: Agency for Healthcare Research and Quality, Center for Financing, Access and Cost Trends. 2011 Medical Expenditure Panel Survey – Insurance Component (MEPS-IC).

Note: Firm size is classified by the number of any type of employee – including full-time, part-time, temporary, and seasonal employees.

Coverage offered by smaller employers does not always share the same attributes as coverage offered by larger employers. One reason is because of how risk is managed.[5] In group insurance, risk is spread among all members of the group. Individuals contribute to a common pool ("risk pool") and contributions from low-risk individuals subsidize the medical costs of higher-risk individuals. The larger the pool, the less likely that costs associated with higher-risk individuals will result in catastrophic financial loss for the entire group. As follows, the smaller the pool the more likely even one individual's use of health care services can adversely affect the entire pool. This means a smaller pool is riskier for an insurer to cover, which can result in the insurer increasing the costs of coverage (either premiums or cost-sharing or both) and/or limiting the benefit package. As a result, small employers may find it difficult to obtain affordable and comprehensive insurance to offer to their employees.

There are additional reasons why smaller employers, as compared to large employers, may find providing health insurance coverage to employees less enticing. For example, the per capita administrative costs for providing coverage might be higher for smaller employers, as there are fewer employees for the administrative costs to be spread among.[6] The result of these and other issues facing smaller employers is that smaller firms are less likely to offer coverage (**Table 1**).

In the nongroup market, risk is not typically pooled in the same way as it is in either the large or small group market. Insurers often decide whether to offer coverage and the terms of that coverage are based on an individual's risk profile (e.g., health status, medical history, pre-existing conditions) rather than on a group's risk profile. Without the stabilizing influence of pooling risk, it can be more difficult for insurers to offer coverage to high-risk individuals. To the extent permitted by law, insurers employ methods, such as excluding coverage for pre-existing conditions and charging higher premiums to individuals based on health status, to address the risk associated with covering high-risk individuals. The use of these tools may not adversely affect individuals with good risk profiles, such as young and healthy individuals. However, an individual with a complex health status (e.g., diabetes) or certain demographic characteristics (e.g., advanced age) can have trouble obtaining and maintaining affordable nongroup coverage that does not exclude benefits and services because of health status or pre-existing conditions.

The various laws that govern private insurance markets influence the characteristics of each market segment. States are the primary regulators of insurance; therefore, they have the authority to impose their own set of requirements on state-licensed carriers in each market. The scope of state laws varies across states, but often state laws and regulations focus on improving access to coverage and/or certain benefits and reducing the cost of coverage. For example, some states have required plans to offer certain benefits, such as infertility treatments and some states have imposed rules on how insurers can vary premiums based on health status and demographic characteristics. The federal government has also passed laws (even prior to ACA) that affect how coverage can be offered and obtained in the private market, and these laws are also often implemented differently across market segments.[7]

ACA Provisions Affecting the Private Health Insurance Market

Private Health Insurance Market Reforms

A number of ACA provisions focus on changing how insurers and sponsors of insurance (e.g., employers) offer coverage. Some of the reforms are already in effect; others will become effective in 2014. Collectively, the market reforms establish federal minimum requirements with respect to access to coverage, premiums, benefits, cost-sharing, and consumer protections, while generally giving states the authority to enforce the reforms and the ability to expand on the reforms. Many of the reforms focus specifically on the small group and nongroup insurance markets to address perceived failures in the markets, such as limited access to coverage and higher costs of coverage, and to provide some parity with the large group market, which may already have many of these features.

Some of the market reforms are new to certain insurance markets; others have been in place in some capacity due to either state or federal laws or both. For example, guaranteed issue is the requirement that a plan accept every applicant for coverage, as long as the applicant agrees to the terms and conditions of the insurance offer (e.g., the premium). In the early 1990s, some states passed laws requiring guaranteed issue in their small group markets, with fewer states adopting types of guaranteed issue laws in their nongroup markets.[8] In 1996, Congress passed the Health Insurance Portability and Accountability Act (HIPAA, P.L. 104-191), which requires guaranteed issue in the small group market in all states. ACA extends these efforts by requiring, beginning in 2014, that all non-grandfathered nongroup and group plans (except those that are self-insured)[9] offer coverage on a guaranteed issue basis (see the shaded **box**).

ACA & Grandfathered Status

Health insurance plans that were in existence (either in the group or nongroup market) and in which at least one person was enrolled on the date of ACA enactment (March 23, 2010) were considered "grandfathered" under ACA.

Individuals enrolled in grandfathered plans may re-enroll in the plan, and family members may join a grandfathered plan, if such enrollment is permitted under the terms of the plan that were in effect on the date of ACA enactment. If the grandfathered plan is a group plan, new members of the group may choose to enroll in the plan.

Grandfathered plans have a unique status under ACA, and they may lose their status if they apply certain changes to benefits, cost-sharing, employer contributions, and access to coverage. As long as a plan maintains its grandfathered status, the plan has to comply with some, but not all ACA provisions.

Table 2. ACA Private Health Insurance Market Reforms Effective Prior to 2014

ACA Provision	Brief Description
Obtaining Health Insurance	
Extension of Dependent Coverage	Applicable plans that offer dependent coverage must make that coverage available to children under age 26
Prohibition of Discrimination Based on Salary	Applicable plans are prohibited from establishing eligibility criteria for full-time employees based on salary
Maintaining Health Insurance	
Prohibition on Rescissions	Applicable plans are prohibited from rescinding coverage except in cases of fraud or intentional misrepresentation
Cost of Purchasing Health Insurance	
Review of "Unreasonable" Rate Increases	Applicable plans must submit a justification for an "unreasonable" rate increase to the HHS Secretary and the relevant state prior to implementation of the increase

ACA Provision	Brief Description
Covered Benefits	
Coverage of Preventive Health Services with No Cost-sharing	Applicable plans are required to provide coverage for preventive health services without cost-sharing
Coverage of Pre-existing Health Conditions – Children	Applicable plans are not allowed to exclude benefits based on pre-existing conditions for children under age 19[a]
Limits on Cost-sharing	
Prohibition on Lifetime Limits	Applicable plans are prohibited from imposing lifetime limits on the dollar value of the essential health benefits (EHB)[b]
Restricted Annual Limits	Applicable plans are restricted from imposing annual limits that fall below a specified dollar threshold on the dollar value of the EHB[c]
Other Consumer Protections	
Medical Loss Ratio (MLR) Requirement	Applicable plans are required to spend a certain amount of premium revenue on medical claims or otherwise provide rebates to policyholders
Standardized Appeals Process	Applicable plans must implement an effective appeals process for coverage determinations and claims
HHS Internet Portal	HHS is required to establish an Internet portal which will allow the public to easily search for health insurance options
Patient Protections	Applicable plans must comply with requirements related to choice of health care professionals and benefits for emergency services
Summary of Benefits and Coverage	Applicable plans must provide a summary of benefits and coverage to individuals that meets the requirements specified by the HHS Secretary
Reporting Requirements Regarding Quality of Care	Applicable plans must annually submit reports to the HHS Secretary and enrollees that address plan quality

Source: CRS analysis of ACA and its implementing regulations.

a. Beginning in 2014, applicable plans will not be able to exclude benefits based on pre-existing conditions for anyone, regardless of age.

b. The essential health benefits (EHB) are certain benefits that all non-grandfathered health plans offered in the nongroup and small group markets will have to cover beginning in 2014. For more information about the EHB, see the "Essential Health Benefits (EHB) Package" section of this report.

c. Beginning in 2014, ACA prohibits annual limits on the dollar value of EHBs.

Table 2 provides a brief overview of the market reforms in ACA that are effective prior to 2014, and **Table 3** describes the market reforms effective in 2014. Together, these tables describe the major market reforms included in

ACA. More specific information, including how the reforms apply to each segment of the private market, can be found in *Private Health Insurance Market Reforms in the Patient Protection and Affordable Care Act (ACA)*, by Annie L. Mach and Bernadette Fernandez.

Table 3. ACA Private Health Insurance Market Reforms Effective in 2014

ACA Provision	Brief Description
Obtaining Health Insurance	
Guaranteed Issue	Applicable plans are required to accept every applicant for health coverage (as long as the applicant agrees to the terms and conditions of the insurance offer)
Nondiscrimination Based on Health Status	Applicable plans are prohibited from basing eligibility for coverage on health status-related factors
Waiting period limitation	Applicable plans cannot establish a waiting period greater than 90 days
Maintaining Health Insurance	
Guaranteed Renewability	Applicable plans must renew individual coverage at the option of the policyholder, or group coverage at the option of the plan sponsor
Cost of Purchasing Health Insurance	
Rating restrictions	Applicable plans can only adjust premiums based on certain ACA-specified factors
Covered Benefits	
Coverage of Pre-existing Health Conditions – All Ages	Applicable plans are prohibited from excluding coverage for pre-existing health conditions for all individuals
Limits on Cost-sharing	
Prohibition on Annual Limits	Applicable plans are prohibited from imposing annual limits on the dollar value of the essential health benefits (EHB)[a]
Other Consumer Protections	
Nondiscrimination Regarding Clinical Trial Participation	Applicable plans cannot prohibit enrollees from participating in approved clinical trials
Nondiscrimination regarding health care providers	Applicable plans are not allowed to discriminate, with respect to participation under the plan, against health care providers acting within the scope of their license or certification

Source: CRS analysis of ACA and its implementing regulations.

a. The essential health benefits (EHB) are certain benefits that all non-grandfathered health plans offered in the nongroup and small group markets will have to cover beginning in 2014. For more information about the EHB, see the "Essential Health Benefits (EHB) Package" section of this report.

Essential Health Benefits (EHB) Package

Both state and federal governments have the authority to require private plans to comply with certain rules and regulations, such as offering certain benefits and services. ACA includes a provision that expands federal requirements with regard to covered benefits and cost-sharing structures.[10] Beginning in 2014, ACA requires that all non-grandfathered plans offered in the nongroup and small group markets (both inside and outside exchanges) offer the EHB package. The EHB package consists of three parts: coverage of the EHB, compliance with specific cost- sharing limitations, and having an actuarial value that corresponds to one of the metal tiers (described below).

ACA does not explicitly define the EHB; rather, it lists 10 broad categories from which benefits and services must be included.[11] ACA requires the HHS Secretary to further define the EHB. In response, the HHS Secretary asked states to select a benchmark plan from four different types of plans. For at least 2014 and 2015, plans that are required to offer the EHB must model their benefits package after the state's benchmark plan. The approach also includes ways for states to supplement the benchmark plans to ensure that benefits and services from all 10 statutorily required categories are represented.[12]

The EHB package includes limits on enrollees' cost-sharing requirements. ACA specifies that the limits work in three ways: (1) prohibition on applying deductibles to preventive health services; (2) prohibition on deductibles, in small group health plans, that are greater than $2,000 for self-only coverage, or $4,000 for any other coverage in 2014 (annually adjusted thereafter); and (3) prohibition on annual out-of-pocket limits that exceed existing limits in the tax code.[13]

Additionally, plans offering the EHB package must meet one of four levels of generosity based on actuarial value. Actuarial value is a summary measure of a plan's generosity, expressed as a percentage of medical expenses estimated to be paid by the issuer for a standard population and set of allowed charges. ACA requires plans that offer the EHB package to meet one of four generosity levels (metal tiers):

- bronze—60% actuarial value;
- silver—70% actuarial value;
- gold—80% actuarial value; and
- platinum—90% actuarial value.

ACA & ACTUARIAL VALUE

Actuarial value is a summary measure of a plan's generosity, expressed as a percentage of medical expenses estimated to be paid by the issuer for a standard population and set of allowed charges. In other words, actuarial value reflects the relative share of cost- sharing that may be imposed. On average, the lower the actuarial value of a plan, the greater the cost-sharing for the enrollee.

It is important to note, however, because actuarial value is a summary measure based on a standard population, it is of varying value to individuals. Its value for an individual depends on how the individual's medical costs align with the costs of the standard population. Also, actuarial value does not take into account aspects of health insurance coverage that may be important to individuals. In particular, actuarial value does not consider the cost of premiums and the adequacy of provider networks, and plans with the same actuarial value do not necessarily include the same set of covered benefits.

Exchanges

ACA requires the establishment of a health insurance exchange in every state.[14] ACA exchanges are marketplaces where individuals and small businesses can shop for and purchase private health insurance coverage.[15] To facilitate the purchase of insurance by these groups, ACA requires the exchanges to have two parts: one where individuals can buy nongroup insurance for themselves (and their families), and a small business health options program (SHOP) exchange that is designed to assist qualified small employers and their employees with the purchase of insurance.[16]

Exchanges are intended to simplify the experience of providing and obtaining coverage in the nongroup and small group markets. They are not intended to supplant the private market outside of exchanges, and individuals and small businesses cannot be compelled to obtain coverage through an exchange. Plans offered in exchanges are generally subject to ACA market reforms and will typically have to offer the essential health benefits (EHB) package. The open enrollment period for exchanges begins October 1, 2013 with coverage beginning in January 2014. Certain individuals purchasing nongroup coverage through an exchange will be eligible to receive financial assistance in the forms of premium tax credits and cost-sharing subsidies.[17]

The Congressional Budget Office (CBO) estimates that in 2014, 7 million nonelderly individuals will obtain coverage through an exchange, and by 2022 that number will increase to 26 million.[18] The following sections briefly describe some features of exchanges.

Exchange Establishment

A state can choose to run its own exchange (state-based exchange) or—if it chooses not to run its own exchange or the federal government determines that it is not ready to run its own exchange— the state will have a federal exchange in one of two forms. The state will either partner with the federal government, allowing the state to manage certain aspects of its exchange while the federal government has authority over the exchange (partnership exchange); or the state will have an exchange that is wholly established and administered by the federal government (federally facilitated exchange).

States interested in running a state-based exchange in 2014 were required to declare their intentions by December 14, 2012. To date, HHS has granted conditional approval[19] for 18 state- based exchanges.[20] States interested in having a partnership exchange in 2014 had until February 15, 2013 to declare their intentions; HHS has conditionally approved seven partnership exchanges.[21] Federal grant funding is available to states to assist in planning and establishing exchanges, and states are able to apply for the grants through 2014. All exchanges, state-based and federal, must be self-sustaining beginning in 2015.

Coverage Offered through an Exchange

ACA requires that plans offered through an exchange are, for the most part, qualified health plans (QHPs). In general, to be certified a QHP, a plan has to offer the EHB package and meet certain standards related to marketing, choice of providers, and plan networks. State-based exchanges will certify plans as QHPs for their exchanges. In federally facilitated exchanges (including partnerships), the federal government will certify QHPs.

ACA allows for some additional types of QHPs—multi-state plans (MSPs), consumer operated and oriented plans (CO-OPs), and child-only QHPs. In general, these plans have to meet many of the same standards as QHPs. Additionally, ACA allows exchanges to offer at least two types of plan that are not required to meet most QHP standards—stand-alone dental plans and catastrophic plans. **Table 4** briefly describes each type of plan that can be offered through an exchange. Unless otherwise noted, the plans may be offered in both the nongroup and small group markets.

Premium Tax Credits

Certain individuals who obtain coverage through an exchange will be eligible to receive health insurance premium tax credits. Premium tax credits are generally available to individuals who

- purchase nongroup coverage through an exchange;
- have household income[22] between 100% and 400% of the federal poverty level (FPL);[23]
- are not eligible for minimum essential coverage;[24] and
- are U.S. citizens (or legally residing in the United States).

To receive a premium tax credit, individuals also must be part of a tax-filing unit, as the credits are administered through federal income tax returns.

While the tax credits are generally directed at individuals who do not have access to coverage outside the nongroup market, certain individuals with access to employer-sponsored insurance (ESI) may be eligible for premium tax credits. An individual who is otherwise eligible for a premium tax credit, but has an offer of ESI, may be eligible for premium tax credits for exchange coverage if the ESI is unaffordable or does not meet a certain minimum value.[25] If this were the case, the individual could purchase nongroup coverage through an exchange with the assistance of a premium tax credit.[26]

The premium tax credits are advanceable, refundable tax credits. This means that tax filers do not have to wait until the end of the tax year to receive the credits (advance payments will go directly to the issuer of coverage), and tax filers may claim the full credit amount regardless of their federal income tax liability (i.e., even filers with no federal income tax liability can claim the credit).The amount of the tax credit will vary from person to person: it depends on the household income of the tax filer (and dependents), the premium for the exchange plan in which the tax filer (and dependents) is (are) enrolled, and other factors. In certain instances, the credit amount may cover the entire premium and the tax filer pays nothing towards the premium. In other instances, the tax filer may be required to pay part of the premium.

Table 4. Types of Health Plans that Can Be Offered Through Exchanges

Type of Plan	Brief Description	Availability to Individuals Eligible for Exchanges
Qualified Health Plans (QHPs)	QHPs are plans that meet certain requirements related to offering the essential health benefits (EHB) package,[a] marketing, choice of providers, plan networks, and other features.	Generally available to all individuals[b]
	An issuer of a QHP must be licensed in a state in which it offers coverage, must agree to offer at least one silver plan and one gold plan, and must comply with all applicable exchange regulations.	
	State-based exchanges will certify QHPs; the federal government will certify QHPs for federally facilitated exchanges and partnership exchanges.	
Multi-state Plans (MSPs)	MSPs are nationally available QHPs that are overseen by the Office of Personnel Management (OPM).	Generally available to all individuals
	In general, MSPs must meet the requirements of QHPs, including being licensed in a state and offering the EHB, as well as other criteria required by OPM.	
	Any MSP deemed certified by OPM will eventually be offered through every exchange, and OPM must offer at least two MSPs in every exchange.[c]	
Consumer Operated and Oriented Plans (CO-OPs)	Plans offered by a CO-OP loan recipient may be deemed eligible to be offered as a QHP in an exchange by the Centers for Medicare & Medicaid Services (CMS).[d]	Generally available to all individuals
	To be deemed a CO-OP QHP, the plans must meet QHP certification requirements, state-specific exchange standards, and all CO-OP program requirements.	

Table 4. (Continued)

Type of Plan	Brief Description	Availability to Individuals Eligible for Exchanges
	In general, CO-OP QHPs must be offered at the silver and gold metal tiers in every exchange that serves the geographic regions in which the CO-OP loan recipient is licensed and intends to provide health insurance coverage.	
Child-only QHPs	Issuers that offer a QHP through an exchange must also offer that plan as a "child-only" plan at the same level of coverage (bronze, silver, gold, or platinum)	Available to individuals less than 21 years of age
Stand-alone Dental Plans	Exchanges must allow issuers to offer stand-alone dental plans if the plans cover pediatric oral services (as specified in the EHB) and if the issuer and plan generally meet the criteria to be certified as a QHP.	Generally available to all individuals
	The dental plans may be offered separate from or in conjunction with a QHP, at issuers' discretion.	
Catastrophic Plans	Issuers may choose to offer catastrophic plans through exchanges.	Available to individuals under 30 years of age, and certain individuals exempt from the individual mandate.
	Catastrophic plans can have actuarial values less than what is required to meet any of the metal tiers (bronze, silver, gold, platinum) but they must include coverage for the EHB and meet certain additional requirements.	Catastrophic plans are only available in the nongroup market.

Source: CRS analysis of ACA and its implementing regulations.

Notes: For more information about coverage available through exchanges, see CRS Report R42663, *Health Insurance Exchanges Under the Patient Protection and Affordable Care Act (ACA)*, by Bernadette Fernandez and Annie L. Mach.

HHS has recently indicated that state-based exchanges may also allow issuers that are Medicaid managed care organizations to offer QHPs in exchanges on a limited-enrollment basis to certain populations. These QHPs would serve as "bridge" plans for individuals who transition from Medicaid and CHIP coverage to an exchange. HHS plans to release additional guidance on these plans. For more information, see Department of Health and Human Services, *Frequently Asked Questions on Exchanges, Market Reforms, and Medicaid*, December 10, 2012.

a. The essential health benefits (EHB) package is described in the "Essential Health Benefits (EHB) Package" section of this report.

b. It should be noted that issuers may offer QHPs outside the exchange as well; if they do, they must agree to charge the same premium for a QHP offered inside and outside the exchange.

c. ACA allows MSPs to phase-in coverage. An MSP must offer coverage in 60% of states the first year it contracts with OPM, 70% of states the second year, 85% of states the third year, and in all states thereafter.

d. Under the CO-OP program, the federal government provides loans to eligible nonprofit entities to help them establish and administer health insurance plans. Prior to 2013, some entities received CO-OP loans, but much of the remaining funding for the CO-OP program has since been rescinded. For more information, see the "Consumer Operated and Oriented Plan (CO-OP) Program" section of this report.

The amount received in premium credits is based on the prior year's income tax returns. These amounts are reconciled in the next year when individuals file a tax return for the actual year in which they received a premium credit. If a tax filing unit's income changed during the year, they may have been eligible for higher or lower amounts of tax credits (depending on whether income decreased or increased). If it is determined that the tax filer should have received a higher amount, this additional credit would be included in their tax refund for the year. If it is determined that the tax filer should have received a lower amount, then the overpayment must be repaid to the federal government as a tax payment, subject to statutorily defined caps on the repayment.[27]

Cost-Sharing Subsidies

Under ACA, some individuals will also be eligible to receive financial assistance in the form of cost-sharing subsidies that go toward cost-sharing expenses, such as coinsurance and co- payments. To be eligible, individuals must be eligible for premium tax credits and enrolled in a silver plan through an exchange.[28]

The cost-sharing subsidies work in two ways. As described earlier, ACA requires each metal tier plan offered through exchanges to have an annual limit on the total amount an enrollee is required to pay out of pocket for use of covered services (see "Essential Health Benefits (EHB) Package"). One way the subsidies work is to reduce the annual limit for individuals with income between 100% and 400% FPL. This form of cost-sharing assistance will reduce the annual limit by two-thirds for qualifying individuals with income between 100% and 200% FPL, by one-half for those with income between 201% and 300% FPL, and by one-third for those with income between 301% and 400% FPL.

The second way that cost-sharing subsidies work is to reduce a plan's cost-sharing requirements to ensure that the plan covers a certain percentage of allowed health care expenses, on average, for the individual. This form of cost-sharing subsidy is available to individuals with income between 100% and 250% FPL, and it will directly affect cost-sharing requirements, such as coinsurance and copayments.

Consumer Operated and Oriented Plan (CO-OP) Program

Some have suggested that the creation of new non-profit consumer governed health insurance companies would benefit the private insurance market because the non-profit cooperatives would return profits directly to their members, or would invest in plan members via lower premiums, lower cost-sharing, expanded benefits, and innovations such as wellness programs, chronic disease management, and integrated care.[29] To facilitate the creation of new health insurance cooperatives, ACA creates the Consumer Operated and Oriented Plan (CO-OP) program.

The HHS Secretary is required to use funds appropriated to the CO-OP program to finance start- up loans and solvency loans for eligible non-profit organizations applying to become CO-OP issuers. Awarded entities are to use the start-up loans for assistance with costs associated with creating the CO-OP, and the solvency loans must be used to help the entity meet state solvency requirements.[30] All loans must be repaid with interest; the start-up loans must be repaid within five years and the solvency loans must be repaid within 15 years (from the date of disbursement).

The HHS Secretary began awarding loans to eligible non-profits in January 2012. As of the date of this report, 24 entities in 24 states have received loans.[31] On January 2, 2013, Congress passed the American Taxpayer Relief Act of 2012 (ATRA, P.L. 112-240), the most recent in a series of laws that rescinded funds from the CO-OP program.[32] ATRA rescinded most of the unobligated CO-OP funds; the only funds remaining for the program must be used to support the 24 entities that have already received CO-OP loans.[33]

The entities that have received loans are required to meet certain standards with regard to the types of health plans they offer. Two-thirds of the plans offered by CO-OP issuers must be qualified health plans (QHPs) offered in the nongroup and small group markets; up to one-third of a CO-OP issuer's plan can be other types of plans, such as Medicaid managed care plans. With regard to how CO-OP issuers are expected to interact with exchanges, CO-OPs must be offered at the silver and gold levels in the nongroup market in each exchange that serves the geographic regions in which the CO-OP loan recipient is licensed and intends to provide health care coverage. CO-OPs must be offered at both the silver and gold levels in the small group market in each SHOP that serves the geographic regions in which the entity is offering coverage, if the CO- OP loan recipient offers at least one plan in the small group market outside an exchange. Accordingly, CO-OPs will be offered in at least the nongroup market in every exchange that shares a geographic region with a CO-OP loan recipient.

Reforms Related to the Allocation of Risk

Beginning in 2014, ACA requires issuers to provide coverage to individuals regardless of health status, medical history, and pre-existing conditions (see **Table 3** for more details). Some individuals will be eligible to receive premium tax credits and cost-sharing subsidies through an exchange, which will increase the attractiveness of coverage by reducing its cost. Also, the individual mandate will be in effect, which requires most individuals to maintain coverage or otherwise pay a penalty.

These provisions are intended to increase the likelihood that individuals will obtain and maintain coverage, but these provisions could also increase the potential for adverse selection. Adverse selection occurs when a large number of individuals who expect or plan for high use of health services enroll in more generous and often more expensive health plans, while simultaneously individuals who expect or plan for low use of health services enroll in more modest plans (both in terms of price and benefits) or choose not to enroll in coverage. Adverse selection can lead to health plans that have risk pools with a large number of high-cost individuals.

ACA establishes three risk programs to help mitigate the potential for adverse selection in the private health insurance market both inside and outside exchanges. Two of the programs, reinsurance and risk corridors, are temporary programs that will be in effect for three years, 2014- 2016. The programs are designed to stabilize the private market until the third program, risk adjustment, is fully developed. The risk adjustment program is a permanent program that begins after the 2014 benefit year. See **Table 5** for more information about the risk programs.

Table 5. Description of Reinsurance, Risk Corridors, and Risk-Adjustment Provisions of ACA

	Reinsurance	Risk Corridors	Risk Adjustment
Description	Reinsurance typically is thought of as insurance for insurers. When issuing policies, an insurer faces the risk that the premiums it collects will not be sufficient to cover its expenses and generate profit. Reinsurance shifts the risk of covering high expenses from the primary insurer to a reinsurer.	Risk corridors refer to a mechanism that adjusts payments to health plans according to a formula based on each plan's actual, allowed expenses in relation to a target amount. If a plan's expenses exceed a certain percentage above the target, the plan's payment is increased. Likewise, if a plan's expenses are at least a certain percentage below the target, the plan's payment is decreased.	Risk adjustment refers to a mechanism that adjusts payments to health plans to take into account the risk that each plan is bearing based on its enrollee population. Plans with enrollment of less than average risk will pay an assessment to the state. States will provide payments to plans with higher than average risk.
	ACA requires all health insurance issuers and third-party administrators of group health plans (including self-insured plans) to contribute to a reinsurance program administered by a nonprofit reinsurance entity. HHS estimates that the contribution rate for 2014 will be $63 per covered life.	Under ACA, HHS must make payments to a QHP issuer that experiences losses that are greater than 3% of the issuer's "projections," while a QHP issuer whose gains are greater than 3% of the issuer's "projections" must remit charges to HHS.	

Table 5. (Continued)

	Reinsurance	**Risk Corridors**	**Risk Adjustment**
	Non-grandfathered individual market plans (inside and outside of exchanges) are eligible for payments from the reinsurance program.	All QHPs in the individual and small group markets (inside and outside of exchanges) must participate in the risk corridor.	All non-grandfathered individual and small group market plans (inside and outside the exchanges, excluding self-insured plans) are subject to risk adjustment.
Objective	Provide funding to plans that incur high costs for enrollees	Limit issuer loss (and gains)	Transfer funds from lowest risk plans to highest risk plans
Goal	Offset a plan's risk associated with high-cost enrollees	Protect against inaccurate rate setting	Protect against adverse selection
Time Frame	Three years (2014-2016)	Three years (2014-2016)	Permanent; begins after end of benefit year 2014

Source: CRS analysis of ACA and its implementing regulations.

Individual Requirement to Maintain Coverage

Beginning in 2014, ACA requires that most individuals maintain health insurance coverage or pay a penalty for noncompliance with the requirement (this provision is often referred to as the "individual mandate"). To comply with the individual mandate, most individuals will need to obtain "minimum essential coverage," which can include employer-sponsored insurance, nongroup coverage, and coverage from federal programs such as Medicare and Medicaid.[34]

Certain individuals are exempt from the mandate, including those with qualifying religious exemptions; those whose household income is less than the filing threshold for federal income taxes for the applicable tax year; those whose required contribution for self-only coverage for a calendar years exceeds 8% of household income;[35] those who receive a hardship exemption from the HHS Secretary; and those who are not lawfully present in the United States.

Individuals are required to pay a penalty for each month of noncompliance with the mandate (provided they are not exempt from the mandate). The annual penalty is the greater of a percentage of "applicable income" or a flat dollar amount assessed on each taxpayer and any dependents.[36] In 2014, the percentage of applicable income is 1.0% and the flat dollar amount is $95. The penalty increases in 2015 and again in 2016. In 2016 and thereafter, the percentage will be 2.5% and the flat dollar amount will be $695 (adjusted for inflation each year after 2016).

It should be noted that ACA caps the penalty for noncompliance; the penalty in any given year cannot exceed the national average premium for bronze-level coverage offered through exchanges (for the relevant family size). Any individuals who are required to pay the penalty but fail to do so will receive a notice from the Internal Revenue Service (IRS). If they still do not pay the penalty, the IRS can attempt to collect the funds by reducing the amount of their tax refund in the future. However, individuals who fail to pay the penalty cannot be subject to any criminal prosecution or penalty for such failure. For example, the IRS cannot file a notice of lien or file a levy on any property for an individual that does not pay the penalty.

The individual mandate is often described as working in conjunction with certain ACA market reforms that will be in effect in 2014: guaranteed issue and renewability, nondiscrimination based on health status, coverage of pre-existing health conditions, and rating restrictions (**Table 3**). Collectively, these reforms require insurers to accept all applicants while concurrently restricting insurers' ability to vary premiums based on an applicant's health status and other characteristics. Because these reforms attempt to provide improved access to coverage for sick individuals, many argue that a provision such as the individual mandate is necessary to encourage healthy individuals to participate in the market so that risk pools are not limited to individuals who are high users of health care services (e.g., individuals who have multiple medical conditions).

Employers

Employers are integral to the provision of private health insurance in the existing market, and ACA includes two provisions that could directly influence an employer's decision to offer health benefits: requirements and penalties related to the offer of insurance, and small business tax credits. Both provisions intend to provide financial incentives for employers to offer health insurance to their employees.

Employer Requirements and Penalties Related to the Offer of Insurance

Beginning in 2014, ACA imposes penalties on certain "large" employers, whether or not they offer health insurance coverage, if a full-time employee receives a premium tax credit toward a plan offered through an exchange. ("Full-time" employees are those working 30 hours per week or more.) For this provision, large employers are those who employed, on average, 50 or more full-time equivalent (FTE) employees in the preceding calendar year.[37]

An employer will not pay a penalty for any part-time worker, even if the part-time employee receives a premium credit. For employers that *do offer* coverage, they will only have to pay a penalty if a full-time worker receives a premium tax credit, which means the worker's self-only coverage from the employer either exceeds 9.5% of household income, or the plan pays for less than 60%, on average, of covered health care expenses. For employers that *do not offer* coverage, they will only have to pay a penalty if a full-time employee receives a premium tax credit.

An employer, regardless of the offer of coverage, pays a penalty if any of its full-time employees obtain coverage through an exchange and receive a premium tax credit. The penalty amount is dependent on whether the employer offers coverage and the total number of full-time employees working for the employer.[38]

Small Business Tax Credit

ACA includes provisions whereby certain small employers can be eligible for a tax credit, provided they contribute a uniform percentage of at least 50% toward their employees' health insurance. The tax credit is available to both non-profit and for-profit employers, but it takes a different form depending on the employer's profit status. The intent of the credit is to encourage small employers to offer coverage for the first time or maintain their offer of coverage.

Small employers can claim the *full* credit amount if they meet the following two criteria:

- The employer has 10 or fewer full-time equivalents (FTEs);[39]
- and the employer's average taxable wages are $25,000 or less.[40]

The credit is phased out as the number of FTEs increases from 10 to 25 and as average employee compensation increases from $25,000 to $50,000. In calculating the number of FTEs, the term "employees" excludes: seasonal workers (working no more than 120 days during the year); a self- employed individual; a 2% shareholder in an S-corporation; a 5% owner of an eligible small business; and someone who is a relation or dependent of these people. Thus, for example, the business will not receive a credit for small business owners or their family members.

For four years, between 2010 and 2013, the *full* credit is available to employers (but subject to the explanation above, employers may only claim part of the credit). Beginning in 2014, the amount of the credit is increased, but it is only available to an employer for two consecutive tax years, and it is only available to employers who obtain coverage through a SHOP exchange. The increased tax credit begins the first year that an employer offers coverage through an exchange. Thus, the small business tax credit is potentially available for a total of six years—the initial credit availability from 2010 through 2013, plus the two-year credit period beginning as early as 2014.

State Options

Many of the provisions discussed to this point are *required* to be implemented under ACA. However, ACA also includes provisions that states *may choose* to implement. The flexibility for states inherent in these "state option" provisions seems intended to allow states to continue programs already in existence or create new programs that may be better-suited to the state's private insurance market.

Basic Health Program

ACA provides states an option to offer coverage to certain low-income individuals through a basic health program (BHP). Beginning in 2015,[41] a state can choose to establish a BHP, which is a health insurance program for individuals under the age of 65 who are not eligible for Medicaid, and it is offered in lieu of these individuals obtaining coverage through an exchange. The BHP would be available to individuals with household income between 133%[42] and 200% FPL,[43] and the BHP coverage must be at least as comprehensive and affordable as what the individuals could have obtained through an exchange. A state that chooses to establish a BHP will receive some funds from the federal government to operate the program.[44]

The BHP in the ACA is modeled after Washington State's Basic Health (BH) plan,[45] a public- private venture that provides subsidized health insurance to certain low-income residents of the state.[46] The BHP provision was included in S. 1796 (111th Congress),[47] a predecessor to ACA. The inclusion of the provision seems to indicate that the BHP is an option for addressing the absence of federal financial assistance for certain populations of low-income individuals. As stated in the Senate Finance Committee report that accompanied S. 1796, "There is no existing Federal law providing direct on-going program financing to the states for health insurance coverage of low income individuals not eligible for Medicaid either under standard criteria or via waivers."[48]

Waiver for State Innovation

ACA allows a state to apply to the HHS Secretary for a waiver of specific requirements with respect to health insurance coverage within that state for plan years beginning on or after January 1, 2017. The state may apply to waive any or all of the following:

- requirements relating to establishment of QHPs;
- requirement for the state to have an exchange;
- requirement to offer premium tax credits and cost-sharing reductions through an exchange;

- requirement for individuals to maintain coverage (individual mandate);
- and the penalties imposed on employers whose employees receive premium tax credits.

For a state to obtain a waiver, the Secretaries (HHS and Treasury) need sufficient information from the state to determine that the state's proposed waiver will: provide benefits that are at least as comprehensive as the EHB; provide coverage and cost-sharing protections against excessive out-of-pocket spending that are at least affordable as the cost-sharing provisions in ACA; provide coverage to at least a comparable number of residents as the provisions of ACA that affect private health insurance would provide; and not increase the federal deficit.

Health Care Choice Compacts

ACA allows two or more states to create a "health care choice compact." The compact would allow the states to enter into an agreement whereby one or more QHPs could be offered in the nongroup market in all states in the compact. In this arrangement, a QHP would only be subject to the laws and regulations of the state in which the plans was issued; however, the issuer of such QHP would be subject to other rules and requirements (e.g., market conduct rules, consumer protection rules) imposed by the state(s) in which the purchaser resides. Additionally, the issuer would either be required to be licensed in each state in the compact or submit to each state's standards for offering insurance, and the issuer must notify all consumers that it may not comply with their state's rules.

A state must have a law that specifically authorizes the state to enter into a compact. The HHS Secretary may approve a compact if it meets certain requirements. The HHS Secretary must promulgate regulations on this provision no later than July 31, 2013; approved compacts cannot go into effect before January 1, 2016.

APPENDIX A. TEMPORARY PROGRAMS

Many ACA provisions that attempt to improve access to coverage are not in place until 2014. To account for this, ACA establishes two temporary programs that are intended to make it easier for certain individuals to obtain coverage prior to implementation of ACA provisions that will ensure their access to coverage. Both temporary programs were implemented shortly after enactment and will end by 2014.

Early Retiree Reinsurance Program (ERRP)

There was some concern that early retirees (those who retire prior to age 65) did not have access to affordable health insurance options. Few employers offer health benefits to early retirees,[49] and individuals are generally not eligible for Medicare until age 65. Coverage in the nongroup market may not be accessible and affordable, depending on the individual's health and economic status.

Many ACA provisions improving access to coverage will be implemented in 2014 and could improve early retirees' coverage options. Until that time, ACA includes the early retiree reinsurance program (ERRP) as one way to address coverage for early retirees.[50] The purpose of the ERRP is to make retiree coverage more affordable for employers to offer and maintain to improve early retirees' access to coverage.

The ERRP program provides reimbursement to sponsors of participating employer-sponsored plans for a portion of the cost of providing health insurance coverage to early retirees (and to the eligible spouses, surviving spouses, and dependents of such retirees).[51] The HHS Secretary reimburses claims for up to 80% of the portion of the cost attributed to such claim that exceeds $15,000 but is not more than $90,000.[52] The reimbursement from the HHS Secretary can only be used to lower costs for the plan or to reduce premium contributions, co-pays, deductibles, co-insurance, or other out-of-pocket costs for plan enrollees.

The program became effective June 1, 2010, and is scheduled to end no later than January 1, 2014. However, the HHS Secretary stopped taking applications for the program on May 5, 2011. The HHS Secretary had authority to stop taking applications for the program based on availability of funding. The HHS Secretary was appropriated $5 billion to carry out the program, and as of February 2012, the ERRP program had provided about $4.7 billion in payments to more than 2,800 employers and other sponsors of retiree coverage.[53]

Pre-existing Condition Insurance Plan (PCIP)

High-risk pools are intended for individuals who cannot obtain or afford health insurance in the private market, primarily because of pre-existing health conditions.[54] States began establishing high-risk pools in the 1970s, and currently 34 states have state-established high-risk pools, and approximately 220,000 individuals are enrolled across the states.[55]

Prior to 2014, ACA's pre-existing condition insurance plan (PCIP) program is intended to supplement existing state-established high-risk pools.[56] Individuals who have been uninsured for at least six months, have been denied coverage because of a pre-existing condition, and are U.S. citizens (or legally residing in the U.S.) are eligible for coverage under a PCIP. Coverage offered in a PCIP must meet certain standards related to the amount enrollees pay toward premiums and cost-sharing requirements. ACA appropriated $5 billion of federal funds to subsidize the program's claims and administrative costs. ACA requires that the program end by 2014, at which time insurers will be prohibited from denying coverage because of an individual's pre-existing health conditions.

States can run the PCIP program or elect to have HHS operate the program in their states. HHS administers the PCIPs in 23 states and the District of Columbia, and 27 states administer their own PCIPs. As of December 31, 2012, approximately 103,160 individuals were enrolled in PCIPs across the states.[57] As of February 16, 2013, the federal government suspended acceptance of new enrollment applications for the PCIPs run by HHS; as of March 2, 2013, the federal government required state-administered PCIPs to also suspend acceptance of new enrollment applications. Both HHS-administered and state-administered PCIPs will continue to cover individuals enrolled prior to the suspension dates (until the program ends in 2014).[58]

Appendix B. Additional ACA Provisions Relating to Benefits and Services

Provisions Related to Abortion

ACA includes provisions that address coverage of abortion services by QHPs offered through exchanges. Under ACA, the issuer of a QHP will determine whether to provide coverage for elective abortions, or abortions for which federal funds appropriated for HHS are permitted,[59] or both. A plan issuer may also choose to not cover either type of abortion. In addition, ACA will permit a state to prohibit abortion coverage in exchange plans by enacting a law with such a prohibition.

Individuals who receive premium credits or cost-sharing subsidies toward purchasing coverage through an exchange will be permitted to purchase an exchange plan that includes coverage for elective abortions. However, to ensure that funds attributable to a premium or cost-sharing subsidy are not used to pay for elective abortion services, ACA prescribes payment and accounting requirements for plan enrollees and issuers.

ACA also provides for conscience protection and the preservation of certain state and federal abortion-related laws. The measure prohibits exchange plans from discriminating against any individual health care provider or health care facility because of its unwillingness to provide, pay for, provide coverage of, or refer for abortions. State laws concerning the prohibition or requirement of coverage or funding for abortions, and state laws involving abortion-related procedural requirements will not be preempted.[60]

Wellness Programs

In the existing private market, group health plans can provide certain incentives for enrollee participation in wellness programs. To do so, group health plans must comply with the wellness program provisions in the Health Insurance Portability and Accountability Act of 1996 (HIPAA, P.L. 104-191). HIPAA generally allows the provision of premium discounts, rebates, or reduced cost-sharing for enrollee participation in wellness programs. HIPAA generally divides wellness programs into two categories:

- "participatory wellness programs" that do not require an individual to satisfy a standard related to a health factor[61] as a condition for obtaining a reward (or do not offer a reward);
- and "health-contingent wellness programs" that require individuals to satisfy a standard related to a health factor in order to obtain a reward.

Participatory wellness programs are compliant with HIPAA as long as participation in the programs is made available to all similarly situated individuals, and HIPAA does not limit the financial incentives these programs can provide. However, health-contingent wellness programs must meet additional requirements to comply with HIPAA. Among these requirements, the reward for such a program cannot exceed 20% of the total cost of self-only coverage under the plan.

Beginning in 2014, ACA modifies this provision of HIPAA by allowing the reward for a health- contingent wellness program to be capped at 30% of the total cost of self-only coverage under the plan. Additionally, ACA gives the Secretaries of HHS, Labor, and the Treasury the discretion to increase the reward up to 50% of the cost of coverage if the increase is determined to be appropriate.

ACA also requires the Secretary of HHS, in consultation with the Secretaries of the Treasury and Labor, to establish a 10-state pilot program no later than July 1, 2014, in which participating states must apply the wellness program provisions to health insurers in the individual market.

End Notes

[1] The intent of health insurance is to minimize the potential financial risk associated with use of health care services. One way to minimize risk in the insurance market is to spread risk among a group of people. This concept is often called risk pooling. A group of individuals contributes to a common pool (risk pool), and contributions from low-cost individuals in the pool (i.e., individuals who use few medical services) subsidize the medical costs of higher-cost individuals in the pool.

[2] ACA includes two provisions that establish temporary programs. Because these provisions are required to end by 2014, they are not discussed in the body of this report. Instead, these provisions, relating to the creation of an early retiree reinsurance program and establishing a pre-existing condition insurance plan, are discussed in **Appendix A**.

[3] The health insurance estimates are from the U.S. Census Bureau's American Community Survey (ACS), 2011. Data are available through American FactFinder, at http://factfinder2.census.gov/faces/nav/jsf/pages/index.xhtml. The percentages include individuals who may have more than one form of insurance.

[4] What constitutes "large" and "small" in the private market varies. Often, for the purpose of state and federal laws, a large employer has more than 50 employees, and a small employer has up to 50 employees. The definitions of "small" and "large" also vary under ACA, but most often ACA defines small as either up to 50 or up to 100 employees.

[5] Risk—the potential for loss—is an underlying concept of insurance. Individuals obtain health insurance to protect themselves against the risk of financial loss in the event of a medical event. To learn more about how risk is managed in the health insurance market, see CRS Report RL32237, *Health Insurance: A Primer*, by Bernadette Fernandez.

[6] Dawn M. Gencarelli, *Health Insurance Coverage for Small Employers*, National Health Policy Forum, April 19, 2005.

[7] For example, federal statutory language on private health insurance can be found in the Employee Retirement Income Security Act (ERISA), the Health Insurance Portability and Accountability Act (HIPAA), and the Public Health Service Act (PHSA).

[8] Mila Kofman and Karen Pollitz, *Health Insurance Regulation by States and the Federal Government: A Review of Current Approaches and Proposals for Change*, Georgetown University Health Policy Institute, April 2006.

[9] A common distinction in the group market is whether plans are fully insured or self-insured. A fully insured plan is one in which the plan sponsor purchases health coverage and the carrier assumes the risk of providing health benefits to the sponsor's enrolled members. A self-insured plans is one in which an entity (e.g., employer or association) provides coverage for its members directly by setting aside funds and paying for health benefits. Under self-insurance, the entity bears the risk for covering medical expenses, and such plans are not subject to state insurance regulations.

[10] It should be noted that ACA includes two additional provisions that relate to whether and how private health plans can offer certain benefits and services. These additional provisions, relating to coverage of abortion services and the offer of wellness programs, are described in **Appendix B**.

[11] The 10 categories are ambulatory patient services; emergency services; hospitalization; maternity and newborn care; mental health and substance use disorder services, including behavioral health treatment; prescription drugs; rehabilitative and habilitative services and devices; laboratory services; preventive and wellness services and chronic disease management; and pediatric services, including oral and vision care.

[12] This approach is described in the final rule, "Patient Protection and Affordable Care Act; Standards Related to Essential Health Benefits, Actuarial Value, and Accreditation," 78 *Federal Register* 12834, February 25, 2013.

[13] The "existing limits" are those that are applicable to high-deductible health plans (HDHPs) that qualify to be paired with health savings accounts (HSAs). In general, an HDHP is an insurance policy with low premiums and a high deductible (the amount that must be paid by an enrollee before the insurer begins to pay for covered services). In 2013, the cost-sharing limit for HSA-qualified HDHPs is $6,250 for single coverage and $12,500 for family coverage. Given that these existing limits are updated annually and this ACA provision does not become effective until 2014, the existing limits in 2014 will likely be different than the 2013 levels.

[14] It should be noted that HHS is currently referring to health insurance exchanges as health insurance *marketplaces*.

[15] Individuals who approach exchanges could also be potentially screened for eligibility for public programs such as Medicaid and the State Children's Health Insurance Program (CHIP). For more information see the "Eligibility and Enrollment" section in CRS Report R42663, *Health Insurance Exchanges Under the Patient Protection and Affordable Care Act (ACA)*, by Bernadette Fernandez and Annie L. Mach.

[16] Before 2016, states will have the option to define "small employers" either as those with 100 or fewer employees or 50 or fewer employees. Beginning in 2016, small employers will be defined as those with 100 or fewer employees. Beginning in 2017, states may allow large employers to obtain coverage through an exchange (but will not be required to do so).

[17] See the "Premium Tax Credits" and "Cost-Sharing Subsidies" sections of this report for more information.

[18] Congressional Budget Office, *The Budget and Economic Outlook: Fiscal Years 2013 to 2023*, February 2013, http://www.cbo.gov/sites/default/files/cbofiles/attachments/43907-BudgetOutlook.pdf.

[19] HHS may also "conditionally approve" state-based exchanges (77 *Federal Register* 18310, March 27, 2012). In its "Blueprint for Approval of Affordable State-based and State Partnership Insurance Exchanges," HHS says it will "utilize conditional approval for state-based exchanges and partnership states where exchange establishment is not complete at the time of Blueprint submission." http://cciio.cms.gov/resources

[20] The following states and DC have received conditional approval to establish a state-based exchange: CA, CO, CT, HI, ID, KY, MD, MA, MN, NV, NM, NY, OR, RI, UT, VT, WA.

For more information, see http://cciio.cms.gov/ resources/factsheets/state-marketplaces.html.

[21] HHS has conditionally approved partnership exchanges in AR, DE, IL, IA, MI, NH, and WV. For more information, see http://cciio.cms.gov/resources

[22] In this instance, household income is "modified adjust gross income" (MAGI). For more information about MAGI and ACA, see CRS Report R41997, *Definition of Income for Certain Medicaid Provisions and Premium Credits in ACA*, coordinated by Janemarie Mulvey.

[23] Lawfully present immigrants with income below 100% of FPL, who are ineligible for Medicaid for the first five years that they are present, are also eligible for premium tax credits. For the purpose of the credits, these individuals will be treated as though their income were exactly 100% of FPL.

[24] According to law, minimum essential coverage includes Medicare Part A; Medicaid; the State Children's Health Insurance Program (CHIP); Tricare; Tricare for Life; a health care program administered by the Department of Veterans Affairs; the Peace Corps program; a local, state, or federal government plan; any plan established by an Indian tribal government; any plan offered in the individual, small group, or large group market; a grandfathered health plan; and any other health benefits coverage (such as a state high risk pool) as recognized by the HHS Secretary in coordination with the Treasury Secretary.

[25] "Affordable" in this context means that the individual's required contribution toward the plan premium for self-only coverage does not exceed 9.5% of their household income. "Minimum value" in this context means that the plan pays for at least 60%, on average, of covered health care expenses.

[26] In this scenario, the individual's employer could be subject to a penalty. See the "Employers" section of this report for more information.

[27] The caps have been modified a few times since ACA enactment, for more information see CRS Report R41137, *Health Insurance Premium Credits in the Patient Protection and Affordable Care Act (ACA)*, by Bernadette Fernandez and Thomas Gabe.

[28] ACA establishes different cost-sharing subsidy eligibility criteria for American Indians and Alaskan Natives. For more information, see CRS Report R41152, *Indian Health Care: Impact of the Affordable Care Act (ACA)*, by Elayne J. Heisler.

[29] Senator Kent Conrad, "FAQ about the Consumer-Owned and -Oriented Plan (CO-OP)," 2010, available at http://conrad.senate.gov/issues

[30] States generally set standards for and monitor state-licensed insurers' financial operations in order to ensure that insurers have adequate reserves to pay policyholders' claims.

[31] The list of entities that have received loans is available at http://cciio.cms.gov/ Archive/Grants/new-loan- program.html.

[32] As enacted, ACA appropriated $6 billion of federal funds for the CO-OP program. The Department of Defense and Full-Year Continuing Appropriations Act, 2011 (P.L. 112-10) rescinded $2.2 billion of the appropriated funding, and the Consolidated Appropriations Act, 2012 (P.L. 112-74) rescinded an additional $400 million from the program. The American Taxpayer Relief Act of 2012 (P.L. 112-240) rescinded nearly all other unobligated CO-OP funds.

[33] ATRA directed the HHS Secretary to create a fund to be used to support all nonprofit insurance issuers who were awarded CO-OP program loans prior to the date of the law's enactment (January 2, 2013). The fund contains 10% of any unobligated CO-OP funds, and the Act rescinded all other unobligated CO-OP funds.

[34] According to law, minimum essential coverage includes Medicare Part A; Medicaid; the State Children's Health Insurance Program (CHIP); Tricare; Tricare for Life; the veteran's health care program; the Peace Corps program; a local, state, or federal government plan; any plan established by an Indian tribal government; any plan offered in the individual, small group, or large group market; a grandfathered health plan; and any other health benefits coverage

(such as a state high risk pool) as recognized by the HHS Secretary in coordination with the Treasury Secretary.

[35] After 2014, the 8% will be adjusted to reflect the excess rate of premium growth above the rate of income growth for the period.

[36] "Applicable income" is defined as the amount by which and individual's household income exceeds the applicable filing threshold for the applicable tax year.

[37] Generally, both full-time and part-time employees are included in the calculation to determine the number of FTEs the employer has, but the calculation does not include full-time seasonal employees who work for up to 120 days during the year.

[38] The penalty is limited to the total number of the employer's full-time employees minus 30. In other words, 30 full- time employees are not counted for the purpose of calculating the penalty.

[39] For the purpose of this provision, FTEs are calculated by dividing the total hours worked by all "employees" (see description below) during the tax year by 2,080 (with a maximum of 2,080 hours for any one employee).

[40] This is calculated by dividing the aggregate amount of wages paid to the "employees" during the year by the number of FTEs (and then rounding to the nearest $1,000).

[41] As enacted, ACA allowed states to establish a BHP beginning in 2014; however, HHS released guidance stating that the program will not be operational and available as a state option until 2015. For more information see, *Questions and Answers: Medicaid and the Affordable Care Act*, available at http://medicaid.gov/State-Resource-Center/FAQ- Medicaid-and-CHIP-Affordable-Care-Act-ACA-Implementation/Downloads/ACA-FAQ-BHP.pdf.

[42] ACA includes a five percentage point income disregard, so the effective limit is 138% FPL.

[43] The BHP would also be available to individuals who are not citizens of the United States, but are lawfully present and are barred from Medicaid because of duration of U.S. residency. These individuals are eligible for a BHP if they otherwise meet the eligibility criteria and have household income not greater than 138% FPL.

[44] The HHS Secretary is required to transfer funds to a state that establishes a BHP in an amount equal to 95% of the premium tax credits and the cost-sharing reductions that would have been provided to the state's BHP enrollees had they been able to obtain coverage through an exchange.

[45] U.S. Congress, Senate Committee on Finance, *America's Healthy Future Act 2009*, report to accompany S. 1796, 111th Cong., 1st sess., October 19, 2009, Report 111-89 (Washington: GPO, 2009).

[46] For more information, see http://www.basichealth.hca.wa.gov/.

[47] S. 1796 never became law; however, some of the language included in the bill was incorporated into ACA.

[48] U.S. Congress, Senate Committee on Finance, *America's Healthy Future Act 2009*, report to accompany S. 1796, 111th Cong., 1st sess., October 19, 2009, Report 111-89 (Washington: GPO, 2009).

[49] Paul Fronstin and Nevin Adams, *Employment-Based Retiree Health Benefits: Trends in Access and Coverage, 1997- 2010*, Employee Benefit Research Institute, No. 377, October 2012, http://www.ebri.org/pdf/briefspdf/EBRI_IB_10- 2012_No377_RetHlth.pdf.

[50] §1102 of ACA.

[51] For this provision, early retirees are individuals aged 55 and older who are not eligible for Medicare and are not active employees of an employer who is maintaining and/or contributing to their employment-based plan.

[52] Amounts are indexed for plan years starting on or after October 1, 2011.

[53] Department of Health and Human Services, *Early Retiree Reinsurance Program: Program Status Update, February 2012*, February 17, 2012, http://cciio.cms.gov/resources

[54] For more information about high-risk pools, see [Archived] CRS Report RL31745, *Health Insurance: State High Risk Pools*, by Bernadette Fernandez.

[55] Enrollment data current as of December 31, 2010; available at http://www.statehealthfacts.org/comparetable.jsp?ind= 602&cat=7.

[56] For more information about the PCIP program, see [archived] CRS Report R41235, *Temporary Federal High Risk Health Insurance Pool Program*, by Bernadette Fernandez.

[57] Department of Health and Human Services, "State by State Enrollment in the Pre-Existing Condition Insurance Plan as of September 30, 2012," press release, November 16, 2012, http://www.healthcare.gov/news/factsheets/2012/11/ pcip11162012a.html.

[58] For more information about the suspensions, see https://www.pcip.gov/.

[59] In addressing the coverage of abortion services by qualified health plans offered through an exchange, ACA refers to the so-called "Hyde Amendment" to distinguish between two types of abortions: abortions for which federal funds appropriated for HHS may be used, and abortions for which such funds may not be used. Under the Hyde Amendment, funds appropriated for HHS may be used to pay for an abortion if a pregnancy is the result of an act of rape or incest, or if a woman's life would be endangered if an abortion were not performed. Such funds may not be used, however, for elective abortions.

[60] For more information about how ACA affects coverage of abortion, see CRS Report R41013, *Abortion and the Patient Protection and Affordable Care Act*, by Jon O. Shimabukuro.

[61] Under HIPAA, "health factors" are: health status, medical conditional (including both physical and mental illness), claims experience, receipt of health care, medical history, genetic information, evidence of insurability (including conditions arising out of act of domestic violence), and disability.

In: Private Health Insurance …
Editor: Duke Riggs

ISBN: 978-1-62948-770-0

Chapter 2

PRIVATE HEALTH PLANS UNDER THE ACA: IN BRIEF*

Bernadette Fernandez and Annie L. Mach

INTRODUCTION

The Patient Protection and Affordable Care Act (ACA, P.L. 111-148), as amended, expands federal private health insurance market requirements, and requires the creation of health insurance exchanges (marketplaces) to provide certain individuals and small employers access to private insurance, among other provisions. While some of ACA's private insurance provisions have already become effective, full implementation begins in 2014 and beyond. Given the breadth of ACA's reforms to the existing private insurance market and creation of new health insurance marketplaces, there is interest in understanding what types of health plans may be offered once these ACA provisions are fully implemented.

This report provides short descriptions of health plans[1] that may be offered inside and outside of exchanges, and includes information about interaction with other selected ACA provisions. The descriptions are displayed in a side-by-side format to facilitate comparison of exchange and non-exchange plans. This report does not attempt to identify all forms of health

* This is an edited, reformatted and augmented version of a Congressional Research Service publication, CRS Report for Congress R43233, prepared for Members and Committees of Congress, from www.crs.gov, dated September 19, 2013.

insurance coverage, but does address all plan types specified under ACA's exchange provisions, as well as major medical plans and certain limited benefit plans offered outside of exchanges. In addition, this report indicates the applicability of ACA's market reforms to plans offered in the private market.

PRIVATE HEALTH PLANS AVAILABLE INSIDE AND OUTSIDE OF ACA EXCHANGES

ACA establishes health insurance exchanges (marketplaces)[2] where qualified individuals and small businesses can "shop" for private health insurance.[3] Exchanges will offer several types of health plans. Exchange plans will provide a comprehensive set of covered benefits (i.e., the "essential health benefits"),[4] except for stand-alone dental plans (which will have to meet a narrow set of benefit requirements). While most of these comprehensive plans will be available to any individual or employer who is qualified to enroll in an exchange, some plans will be available only to specific subpopulations (for example, child-only plans). Finally, some plans offered in exchanges may also be offered outside of exchanges.[5]

Exchanges are not intended to be substitutes or replacements for the existing private health insurance market. Prior to ACA, private entities sold health plans to individuals, families, and groups (e.g., employers). This preexisting private market will continue after full implementation of ACA. Thus, ACA envisions the availability of private plans both inside of exchanges, and outside of them in the ongoing market. Moreover, ACA's private insurance requirements establish a federal floor with respect to health insurance regulation. Individual states will continue to regulate health insurers in their respective states, and may apply state-only insurance requirements, as long as such requirements do not prevent the application of ACA's market reforms.[6] Depending on the specific state-only requirements, such reforms may apply to plans inside exchanges as well as outside.

Table 1 provides summaries of the following plan types: qualified health plans, child-only plans, multi-state plans, plans offered through health cooperatives, catastrophic and other high-deductible health plans, plans that provide limited benefits (such as dental-only and other types), plans offered through group and nongroup markets, grandfathered plans, self-funded plans, union plans, and retiree-only plans. The summaries denote whether such plans may be offered inside and/or outside of exchanges, and indicate if individuals enrolled in such plans may avail themselves of the premium tax credits and cost-sharing subsidies established under ACA,[7] and whether enrollment in a given plan meets the requirements to comply with ACA's individual mandate.[8] While each plan type is described in a separate row, these categories are not mutually exclusive. For example, a high-deductible health plan may be offered as a plan in the nongroup, small group, or large group market.[9]

Table 1. Private Health Plans Available Inside and Outside of ACA Exchanges

Types of Health Plans	Inside ACA Exchanges	Outside ACA Exchanges
Qualified Health Plans (QHPs)	QHPs will meet all applicable private market reforms and provide comprehensive coverage, such as covering the essential health benefits (EHBs).[a] Qualified individuals who are enrolled in QHPs through an individual exchange (not a SHOP exchange)[b] may be eligible to receive premium tax credits and cost-sharing subsidies. Individuals enrolled in QHPs will have complied with ACA's individual mandate.	QHPs purchased outside the exchanges must meet all the same requirements as exchange QHPs, but individuals enrolled in QHPs outside of exchanges are not eligible to receive premium tax credits or cost-sharing subsidies. Individuals enrolled in QHPs will have complied with ACA's individual mandate.
Child-only Plans	An insurance company that offers a QHP through an exchange must also offer a child-only plan at the same level of coverage (bronze, silver, gold, or platinum)[c] as that QHP. Exchange child-only plans are available to individuals who are less than 21 years of age. Qualified individuals who are enrolled in child-only plans through an exchange may be eligible for premium tax credits and cost-sharing subsidies. Individuals enrolled in child-only plans will have complied with ACA's individual mandate.	Child-only plans offered outside the exchanges are not required to limit the offer of such plans to individuals under age 21. Individuals enrolled in child-only plans outside the exchanges are not eligible to receive premium tax credits or cost-sharing subsidies. Individuals enrolled in child-only plans will have complied with ACA's individual mandate.

Table 1. (Continued)

Types of Health Plans	Inside ACA Exchanges	Outside ACA Exchanges
Multi-State Plans (MSPs)	MSPs are QHPs that will eventually be available through every exchange, so that individuals and small businesses will have access to these plans, regardless of where they live. Qualified individuals who are enrolled in an individual MSP may be eligible for premium tax credits and cost-sharing subsidies. Individuals enrolled in MSPs will have complied with ACA's individual mandate.	N/A
Health Cooperatives	Health cooperatives who receive loans under the "CO-OP" program established under ACA, and are certified to participate in exchanges, must offer QHPs through individual exchanges (and may also offer plans through SHOP exchanges). CO-OPs must ensure that individual and small group QHPs account for at least 2/3 of their business. Qualified individuals who are enrolled in a CO-OP QHP through an individual exchange may be eligible for premium tax credits and cost-sharing subsidies. Individuals enrolled in CO-OP plans will have complied with ACA's individual mandate.	The coverage offered by health cooperatives outside of exchanges will be substantially the same as the CO-OP coverage offered in exchanges. However, cooperatives that only operate outside of exchanges are not subject to the 2/3 rule. Individuals enrolled in cooperatives outside the exchanges are not eligible to receive premium tax credits or cost-sharing subsidies. Individuals enrolled in plans offered through cooperatives will have complied with ACA's individual mandate.
Catastrophic and other High Deductible Health Plans (HDHPs)	"Catastrophic" plans[d] are available only to individuals under 30 years of age and those who have a hardship exemption from the individual mandate.[e] These individual plans do not have to meet the actuarial value standards specified for QHPs, but they must include coverage for the EHBs. Premium tax credits and cost-sharing subsides may not be used	Catastrophic plans offered outside the exchanges must comply with the same requirements that apply to catastrophic plans offered in the exchanges. Premium tax credits or cost-sharing subsidies

Types of Health Plans	Inside ACA Exchanges	Outside ACA Exchanges
	toward these plans. Individuals enrolled in catastrophic plans will have complied with ACA's individual mandate. A high-deductible health plan that does not meet the specific criteria to be a catastrophic plan may be offered in the exchanges, as long as the HDHP meets the standards applicable to one of the various QHPs that may be offered through exchanges. As long as HDHPs meet all applicable exchange requirements, premium tax credits and cost-sharing subsidies may be used toward these plans. Individuals enrolled in high-deductible plans will have complied with ACA's individual mandate.	may not be used toward catastrophic plans outside the exchanges. Individuals enrolled in catastrophic plans will have complied with ACA's individual mandate. Other HDHPs may be offered outside of the exchanges, as long as they meet all applicable insurance standards. These HDHPs may be broadly offered to individuals and groups. Premium tax credits or cost-sharing subsidies may not be used toward HDHPs outside the exchanges. Individuals enrolled in high-deductible plans will have complied with ACA's individual mandate.
Stand-alone Dental Plans	Dental-only plans may be offered in exchanges, either as stand-alone plans or in conjunction with a QHP, as long as the dental plans include pediatric dental benefits. Premium tax credits and cost-sharing subsides may not be used toward dental-only plans. Enrollment only in a stand-alone dental plan does not meet ACA's individual mandate.	Dental-only plans may be offered outside the exchanges. Such plans are not required to offer pediatric dental benefits as included in EHBs. Premium tax credits and cost-shari subsides may not be used toward dental-only plans. Enrollment only in a stand-alone dental plan does not meet ACA's individual mandate.
Nongroup, Small Group, and Large Group Plans (non-ACA established plans)[f]	N/A	Insurance companies may continue to offer plans in the nongroup, small group, and large

Table 1. (Continued)

Types of Health Plans	Inside ACA Exchanges	Outside ACA Exchanges
		group markets. Plans must comply with applicable state and federal health insurance requirements, including ACA market reforms.[g] Premium tax credits or cost-sharing subsidies may not be used toward plans outside the exchanges. Individuals enrolled in plans offered through the nongroup, small group, or large group markets will have complied with ACA's individual mandate.
Grandfathered Plans[h]	N/A	Existing health insurance coverage in which at least one person has been enrolled on or before March 23, 2010. Grandfathered plans are exempt from the majority of ACA's market reforms. Premium tax credits or cost-sharing subsidies may not be used toward grandfathered plans. Individuals enrolled in grandfathered plans will have complied with ACA's individual mandate.
Self-funded Plans	N/A	Health benefits are provided directly by the organization sponsoring coverage, so technically this is not insurance. Such organizations bear the risk; i.e., they are responsible for paying all covered medical expenses. Premium tax credits or

Types of Health Plans	Inside ACA Exchanges	Outside ACA Exchanges
		cost-sharing subsidies may not be used toward self-funded plans. Individuals enrolled in self-funded plans will have complied with ACA's individual mandate. Self-funded plans are also referred to as self-insured plans.
Union Plans[i]	N/A	Union plans are collectively bargained and maintained by one or more employers. Such plans are exclusively available to unionized employees and their dependents. Premium tax credits or cost-sharing subsidies may not be used toward union plans. Individuals enrolled in plans offered through unions will have complied with ACA's individual mandate.
Retiree-only Plans	N/A	Health plans offered only to retirees of a given employer sponsoring such health benefits are exempt from federal health insurance requirements, including ACA.[j] Premium tax credits or cost-sharing subsidies may not be used toward retiree-only plans. Individuals enrolled in retiree-only plans offered through former employers will have complied with ACA's individual mandate.

Table 1. (Continued)

Types of Health Plans	Inside ACA Exchanges	Outside ACA Exchanges
Vision Plans, Ancillary Insurance Products, and Limited-benefit Plans	N/A[k]	Vision-only plans, ancillary insurance products, and limited-benefit plans are all allowed to be offered outside of exchanges. Premium tax credits or cost-sharing subsidies may not be used toward plans that provide only a single set of or limited benefits. Enrollment only in a plan that provides less than comprehensive benefits would not meet ACA's individual mandate.

Source: CRS analysis of ACA, other applicable federal requirements, and state health insurance standards.

Notes: The plan headers are not mutually exclusive. For example, a high-deductible health plan may be offered as a plan in the nongroup, small group, or large group market. The plans for which premium tax credits and cost-sharing subsidies may be used assume the individual/family meets all eligibility criteria (e.g., income requirement). The plans for which enrollment would satisfy the individual mandate assume the coverage has met all applicable federal and state health insurance requirements to be offered in the private market, whether inside or outside of exchanges. The plans for which sole enrollment would not satisfy the individual mandate assume such coverage has not been recognized by the Secretary of Health and Human Services as meeting the individual mandate requirements.

[a] QHP is a new type of comprehensive health plan, established under ACA, that is subject to standards related to marketing, choice of providers, plan networks, essential benefits, cost-sharing limits, and other features, as specified under §§1301-1302 of ACA. For additional information about QHPs, see CRS Report R42663, Health Insurance Exchanges Under the Patient Protection and Affordable Care Act (ACA).

[b] The Small Business Health Option Program (SHOP) exchange will help qualified small employers select one or more QHPs to offer to their employees. Employers will contribute to the employee's premium and plan holders will not be eligible for premium tax credits or cost-sharing subsidies.

[c] The precious metal designations refer to specific ACA standards related to actuarial value. Actuarial value (AV) is a summary measure of a plan's generosity, expressed as the percentage of medical expenses estimated to be paid by the insurer for a standard population and set of allowed charges. In other words, the higher the percentage, the lower the cost-sharing, on average. Each precious metal corresponds to a specific actuarial value: Bronze (actuarial value of 60%), Silver (70%), Gold (80%), and Platinum (90%).

[d] Prior to ACA, the term catastrophic was used generically to refer to high-deductible health plans (HDHPs). Under ACA, catastrophic has a specific meaning that distinguishes such a plan from other HDHPs.

[e] ACA mandates that most individuals have insurance coverage, but it provides a number of exemptions, one of them being for individuals experiencing a financial hardship.

[f] The private health insurance market is often described as containing three segments: the nongroup (individual), small group, and large group markets. The term "nongroup" refers to health insurance coverage offered to individuals (and potentially their dependents) that is not in connection with a group health plan (which is sponsored by an employer or employee organization, such as a union).

[g] While insurers that participate in exchanges and plans offered by such insurers are required to meet exchange-specific requirements, they also are subject to the same "market reforms" that apply to plans outside of exchanges. For additional information about these reforms, see CRS Report R42069, Private Health Insurance Market Reforms in the Patient Protection and Affordable Care Act (ACA), and CRS Report R43048, Overview of Private Health Insurance Provisions in the Patient Protection and Affordable Care Act (ACA).

[h] See CRS Report R41166, Grandfathered Health Plans Under the Patient Protection and Affordable Care Act (ACA).

[i] ACA did not amend how union plans are negotiated, funded, or administered. However, certain ACA provisions may apply to the coverage offered through union plans. For example, union plans that are offered to active workers are subject to the requirement to extend dependent coverage to children under age 26. For a discussion regarding the applicability of ACA to union plans, see U.C. Berkeley Labor Center, The Affordable Care Act: A Guide for Union Negotiators, August 2012, http://laborcenter.berkeley.edu/ healthpolicy/acaguide12.pdf.

[j] This exemption pre-dates ACA. For a discussion about this exemption, see the Appendix of CRS Report R41166, Grandfathered Health Plans Under the Patient Protection and Affordable Care Act (ACA).

[k]. All exchange plans, except for stand-alone dental plans, are required to offer EHBs. If exchange plans lack pediatric vision benefits, such plans must supplement those benefits through the addition of the entire set of pediatric vision benefits that are covered through either the largest vision plan under the Federal Employee Dental and Vision Insurance Program (FEDVIP), or the largest separate State Children's Health Insurance Plan (CHIP) in the state. For more information about CHIP, see CRS Report R40226, P.L. 111-3: The Children's Health Insurance Program Reauthorization Act of 2009. Vision plans and ancillary insurance products (e.g., life or disability insurance) cannot be offered as stand-alone plans through an exchange, but an exchange may provide basic information about these types of plans on its website. For more information about exchanges and vision plans and other ancillary insurance products, see CMS's "Frequently Asked Questions on Reuse of Exchange for Ancillary Products," http://www.cms.gov/ CCIIO/

Resources/Files/ Downloads/ancillary-product-faq-03-29-2013.pdf. It is unclear from this guidance whether "ancillary insurance products" could include limited-benefit plans as they are being defined in this report. Limited-benefit plans (e.g., plans that include benefits that treat only a single disease) cannot be offered through an exchange. Enrollment only in a plan that provides less than comprehensive benefits would not meet ACA's individual mandate.

ACA MARKET REFORMS APPLICABLE TO PRIVATE HEALTH PLANS

ACA establishes federal requirements that apply to private health insurance. The reforms affect insurance offered to groups and individuals, impose requirements on sponsors of coverage (such as employers), and, collectively, establish a federal floor with respect to access to coverage, premiums, benefits, cost-sharing, and consumer protections. While some of these market reforms are new at the federal level, many of ACA's reforms have already been enacted in some states, with great variation in scope and specificity of those state requirements.[10] Some of ACA's market reforms have already been implemented, while others become effective in 2014.

Given the breadth of types of health coverage, ACA market reforms may affect health plans differently. Some provisions will apply uniformly while others may be more specific to a type of plan. For instance, nearly all plans are required to extend dependent coverage to children under the age of 26. In contrast, several plan types are exempt from the requirement to cover essential health benefits: grandfathered plans, large group plans,[11] self-funded plans, retiree-only plans, and plans that provide limited benefits.

Table 2 indicates the applicability of select ACA market reforms[12] to different types of health coverage; plan types are column headers, while reforms are row headers. The first four market reforms listed in the table became effective prior to 2014 (shaded rows); the remaining reforms will become effective in 2014. For table cells where a market reform applies to some but not all categories within a plan type, the exceptions are described in table notes. For example, the minimum medical loss ratio requirement applies to certain categories of grandfathered plans, but not all grandfathered plans. The category of grandfathered plans that is exempt from this requirement is described in a table note. Other exemptions are likewise indicated in table notes.

Table 2. Applicability of Selected ACA Market Reforms to Private Health Plan Types

	Plans Offered Only Inside Exchanges	Plans Offered Both Inside and Outside Exchanges						Plans Offered Only Outside Exchanges				
ACA Market Reforms	Multi-State Plans (MSPs)	Qualified Health Plans (QHPs)	Child-only Plans	Health Coop-eratives	Catastrophic and other High Deductible Health Plans (HDHPs)	Stand-alone Dental Plans	Nongroup, Small Group, and Large Group Plans (non-ACA)	Grand-fathered Plans	Self-funded Plans	Union Plans	Retiree-only Plans	Vision Plans, Ancillary Insurance Products, and Limited-benefit Plans
Prohibition on Lifetime Dollar Limits	√	√	√	√	√	—	√	√	√	√	—	—
Coverage of Preventive Health Services with No Cost-Sharing	√	√	√	√	√	—	√a	—	√a	√a	—	—
Extension of Dependent Coverage Minimum Medical Loss Ratio (MLR)	√ √ √	√ √ √	√ √ √	√ √ √	√ √b √d	— — Dental benefits only	√ √c	√ √c	√ —	√ √c	— —	— —

Table 2. (Continued)

ACA Market Reforms	Plans Offered Only Inside Exchanges	Plans Offered Both Inside and Outside Exchanges						Plans Offered Only Outside Exchanges				
	Multi-State Plans (MSPs)	Qualified Health Plans (QHPs)	Child-only Plans	Health Coop-eratives	Catastrophic and other High Deductible Health Plans (HDHPs)	Stand-alone Dental Plans	Nongroup, Small Group, and Large Group Plans (non-ACA)	Grand-fathered Plans	Self-funded Plans	Union Plans	Retiree-only Plans	Vision Plans, Ancillary Insurance Products, and Limited-benefit Plans
Essential Health Benefits (EHBs)							√e	—	—	√e	—	—
Minimum Actuarial Value	√	√	√	√	√[d]	—	√[e]	—	—	√[e]	—	—
Prohibition on Annual Dollar Limits	√	√	√	√	√	—	√[f]	√[g]	√	√	—	—
Non-discrimination based on Health Status	√	√	√	√	√	—	√[a]	—	√[a]	√[a]	—	—
Guaranteed Issue and Guaranteed	√	√	√	√	√[b]	—	√[h]	—	—	√h	—	—

ACA Market Reforms	Plans Offered Only Inside Exchanges	Plans Offered Both Inside and Outside Exchanges						Plans Offered Only Outside Exchanges				
	Multi-State Plans (MSPs)	Qualified Health Plans (QHPs)	Child-only Plans	Health Coop-eratives	Catastrophic and other High Deductible Health Plans (HDHPs)	Stand-alone Dental Plans	Nongroup, Small Group, and Large Group Plans (non-ACA)	Grand-fathered Plans	Self-funded Plans	Union Plans	Retiree-only Plans	Vision Plans, Ancillary Insurance Products, and Limited-benefit Plans
Renewal												
Coverage of Preexisting Health Conditions (Regardless of Age)	√	√	√	√	√	—	√[f]	√[g]	√	√	—	—
Rating Restrictions	√	√	√	√	√[d]	—	√[e]	—	—	√[e]	—	—

Source: CRS analysis of ACA.

Notes: The plan headers are not mutually exclusive. For example, a high-deductible health plan may be offered as a plan in the nongroup, small group, or large group market. Shaded area indicates ACA market reforms with a pre-2014 effective date. Unshaded area indicates ACA market reforms with a 2014 effective date. For descriptions of these market reforms, see CRS Reports CRS Report R42069, Private Health Insurance Market Reforms in the Patient Protection and Affordable Care Act (ACA), and CRS Report R43048, Overview of Private Health Insurance Provisions in the Patient Protection and Affordable Care Act (ACA).

[a] Grandfathered plans are exempt.

[b] Self-funded HDHPs are exempt.

[c] Self-funded plans are exempt.

[d] HDHPs offered in the large group market or that are self-funded are exempt.

[e] Large group plans, grandfathered plans, and self-funded plans are exempt.

[f] Grandfathered nongroup plans are exempt.

[g] Nongroup plans are exempt.

[h] Grandfathered plans and self-funded plans are exempt.

End Notes

[1] It is commonplace within the insurance industry to refer to consumers using two different terms—policyholders (for nongroup coverage) and enrollees (for group coverage)—in order to distinguish the type of health coverage a given consumer has. For the sake of simplicity, this report will refer to consumers as enrollees, even if they have coverage through the nongroup market. Likewise, coverage will be referred to as a health plan, even if the coverage is provided through the nongroup market.

[2] For a comprehensive discussion about ACA exchanges, see CRS Report R42663, Health Insurance Exchanges Under the Patient Protection and Affordable Care Act (ACA).

[3] Before 2016, states will have the option to define "small employers" either as those with 100 or fewer employees or 50 or fewer employees. Beginning in 2016, small employers will be defined as those with 100 or fewer employees. Beginning in 2017, states may allow large employers to obtain coverage through an exchange (but will not be required to do so).

[4] ACA specifies 10 broad benefit categories which must be included in essential health benefits: (1) ambulatory patient services; (2) emergency services; (3) hospitalization; (4) maternity and newborn care; (5) mental health and substance use disorder services, including behavioral health treatment; (6) prescription drugs; (7) rehabilitative and habilitative services and devices; (8) laboratory services; (9) preventive and wellness and chronic disease management; and (10) pediatric services, including oral and vision care.

[5] Plans that are offered both inside and outside of exchanges must charge the same premium. In addition, ACA allows the types of health plans that are currently offered in the private market to continue to be offered in 2014 and beyond, as long as those other plan types comply with applicable federal and state law.

[6] §1321(d) of ACA.

[7] ACA provides two forms of financial assistance to certain individuals and families who enroll in exchange plans: tax credits to go toward the purchase of insurance and cost-sharing subsidies to go towards costs associated with use of covered services. For additional information about this financial assistance, see CRS Report R41137, Health Insurance Premium Credits in the Patient Protection and Affordable Care Act (ACA).

[8] ACA includes a mandate for most individuals to have health insurance or potentially pay a penalty for noncompliance. ACA specifies a broad range of sources of comprehensive coverage that will meet this requirement. In addition, the Secretary of Health and Human Services is authorized under ACA to recognize other coverage as meeting this requirement. For additional information about the individual mandate, see CRS Report R41331, Individual Mandate and Related Information Requirements under ACA.

[9] The private health insurance market is often described as containing three segments: the nongroup (individual), small group, and large group markets. The term "nongroup" refers to health insurance coverage offered to individuals (and potentially their dependents) that is not in connection with a group health plan (which is sponsored by an employer or employee organization, such as a union).

[10] For more information about the market reforms, see CRS Reports CRS Report R42069, Private Health Insurance Market Reforms in the Patient Protection and Affordable Care Act (ACA), and CRS Report R43048, Overview of Private Health Insurance Provisions in the Patient Protection and Affordable Care Act (ACA).

[11] However, states have the option to allow large groups to purchase insurance offered through exchanges. All exchange plans (with the exception of stand-alone dental plans) are required to offer EHBs.

[12] The table considers most market reforms included in ACA. However, there are other federal and state requirements that may also apply to these various plans, including some preexisting requirements that are similar to ACA provisions. For example, ACA includes a guaranteed issue provision. Such a requirement existed, prior to ACA, at the federal level for certain types of plans and in certain states.

In: Private Health Insurance …
Editor: Duke Riggs

ISBN: 978-1-62948-770-0

Chapter 3

PRIVATE HEALTH INSURANCE MARKET REFORMS IN THE PATIENT PROTECTION AND AFFORDABLE CARE ACT (ACA)*

Annie L. Mach and Bernadette Fernandez

SUMMARY

The private health insurance provisions in the Patient Protection and Affordable Care Act (ACA, P.L. 111-148, as amended) include market reforms that impose requirements on private health insurance plans. Such reforms relate to the offer, issuance, generosity, and pricing of health plans, among other requirements.

ACA's market reforms largely focus on the individual and small group health insurance markets, and in this report the reforms have been grouped by effective dates: "immediate" market reforms that become effective *prior* to the full implementation date of ACA, and reforms that become effective *on* the full implementation date (January 1, 2014).

ACA requires implementation of a number of reforms prior to its full implementation date (i.e., prior to plan years beginning on or after January 1, 2014). "Immediate" reforms include a process to review unreasonable rate increases; an Internet portal to assist consumers in identifying coverage options; prohibition on lifetime limits and restriction of annual limits; the prohibition on rescissions; coverage of preventive

* This is an edited, reformatted and augmented version of Congressional Research Service, Publication No. R42069, dated February 5, 2013.

health services with no cost-sharing; extension of dependent coverage; prohibition of discrimination based on salary; standards related to medical loss ratios and rebates to plan participants; appeals processes; coverage of preexisting health conditions for children; patient protections; uniform explanation of coverage documents; and reporting requirements regarding quality of care.

Market reforms effective beginning in 2014 include nondiscrimination based on health status; guaranteed issue and guaranteed renewability; coverage of preexisting health conditions (regardless of age); nondiscrimination regarding clinical trial participation; rating restrictions; waiting period limitation; and nondiscrimination regarding health care providers.

This report provides background information about the private health insurance market, including market segments and regulation. It describes each ACA market reform and notes any major implementation activity that has occurred (e.g., issuance of final rule from a department such as Health and Human Services). The appendices of the report provide additional information about the status of regulations relating to each reform (Appendix A) and how the reforms apply to the different market segments and health plans (Appendix B).

INTRODUCTION

The Patient Protection and Affordable Care Act (ACA, P.L. 111-148, as amended) includes reforms of the health insurance market that impose requirements on private health insurance plans.[1] Such reforms relate to the offer, issuance, generosity, and pricing of health plans, among other requirements. Certain reforms also require the participation of public agencies and officials, such as the Secretary of Health and Human Services (hereinafter, the Secretary), in order to facilitate administrative or operational functions.

This report provides background information about the private health insurance market, including market segments and regulation. It describes each ACA market reform and notes any major implementation activity that has occurred (e.g., issuance of final rule from a Department such as Health and Human Services).[2] The appendices of the report provide additional information about the status of regulations relating to each reform (Appendix A) and how the reforms apply to the different market segments and health plans (Appendix B).

BACKGROUND

Health Insurance Markets

The private health insurance market is often characterized as having three segments—the large group, small group, and individual markets. Insurance sold in the large and small group markets refers to health plans offered through a plan sponsor, typically an employer.[3] Typically, large groups have more than 50 workers, and small groups have 50 or fewer workers. However, ACA implements specific definitions of large and small groups that affect many provisions discussed in this report. Prior to 2016, states have the option to define "small employers" as those who employ 100 or fewer employees or 50 or fewer. Beginning in 2016, small employers will be defined as those with 100 or fewer workers.[4] The individual (nongroup) market refers to insurance policies offered to individuals and families buying insurance on their own (i.e., not through a plan sponsor).

State and Federal Regulation

States are the primary regulators of the business of health insurance, as codified by the 1945 McCarran-Ferguson Act (15 U.S.C. §§1011 *et seq.*). Each state has a large, unique set of rules that apply to state-licensed insurance carriers and the plans they offer.[5] Such rules are broad in scope and address a variety of issues, such as the legal structure and organization of insurance issuers (e.g., licensing requirements), business practices (e.g., marketing rules), market conduct (e.g., capital and reserve standards), nature of insurance products (e.g., benefit mandates), and consumer protections (e.g., plan disclosure requirements), among others.

In addition to the state regulation of insurance, the federal government has established federal standards applicable to health coverage and imposes requirements on state-licensed insurance carriers and sponsors of health benefits (e.g., employers). The federal regulation of health coverage is particularly salient with respect to health benefits provided through employment.[6]

ACA follows the model of federalism which has been employed in prior federal reform efforts (e.g., Health Insurance Portability and Accountability Act of 1996). In other words, while ACA establishes many federal rules, the states have primary responsibility for monitoring compliance with and enforcement of such rules. In addition, states may impose additional requirements on insurance carriers and the health plans they offer, provided that the state requirements neither conflict with federal market reforms nor prevent the implementation of such reforms.

ACA Market Reforms

ACA establishes federal requirements that apply to private health insurance. The reforms affect insurance offered to groups and individuals, impose requirements on sponsors of coverage, and, collectively, establish a federal floor with respect to access to coverage, premiums, benefits, cost-sharing, and consumer protections. While such market reforms may be new at the federal level, many of ACA's reforms had already been enacted in some form in some states, with great variation in scope and specificity across the states.

Most of ACA's market reforms become effective in 2014, but a number are already effective.[7] The following sections describe reforms that are effective "immediately" and reforms that are effective for plan years beginning on or after January 1, 2014. The descriptions of the reforms include information from the statute and from regulations, where pertinent. More information about the status of regulations relating to each reform is available in Appendix A.

The application of reforms across types of plans is not uniform. Often reforms apply differently to health plans according to the market segment in which the plan is offered and whether the plan has grandfathered status.[8] Moreover, for certain plans the ACA market reforms, as well as other federal health reforms, do not apply. For example, retiree-only health plans are not required to comply with federal health insurance requirements, such as the dependent coverage requirement.[9] In the text of this report the term "plan" is used generally; for information as to the specific types of plans (i.e., a grandfathered plan in the large group market) to which a reform applies, see Appendix B.

"Immediate" Market Reforms

ACA requires implementation of a number of reforms prior to its full implementation date (i.e., prior to plan years beginning on or after January 1, 2014). The ACA term "immediate" refers to the legal effective date of the provision. The actual implementation date, however, may not be immediate due to the time required to make the provision operational.[10]

The following "immediate" reforms are discussed in this section:

- rate review;
- Internet portal to assist consumers in identifying coverage options;
- prohibition on lifetime limits and restriction of annual limits;
- prohibition on rescissions;
- coverage of preventive health services with no cost-sharing;
- extension of dependent coverage;
- prohibition of discrimination based on salary;
- medical loss ratio (MLR);
- appeals process;
- coverage of preexisting health conditions for children;
- patient protections;
- uniform explanation of coverage documents; and
- reporting requirements regarding quality of care.

Rate Review

The Secretary must, in conjunction with the states, establish a process for the annual review of "unreasonable" increases in health insurance rates beginning in the 2010 plan year. Plans are required to submit to the Secretary, and the relevant state, a justification for an unreasonable rate increase prior to implementation.[11]

The intent of the rate review program is to ensure that all proposed rate increases in the small group and individual markets that meet or exceed a specified threshold are reviewed by a state or the Centers for Medicare & Medicaid Services (CMS) to determine whether they are unreasonable.[12] Health plans subject to review are required to submit to the Department of Health and Human Services (HHS) and the relevant state a justification for the proposed rate increase prior to implementation of the premium, and HHS will publicly disclose the information.

For the first year of the rate review program (plan years beginning on or after September 1, 2011), a proposed rate increase was considered unreasonable if the increase was 10% or more (over a 12-month period beginning on September 1). Going forward, state-specific thresholds may be established. If no state-specific threshold is established, the 10% threshold will continue to be in effect.[13] Note that ACA's rate review process does not establish federal authority to deny implementation of a proposed rate increase.

(This is a "sunshine" provision designed to publicly expose rate increases determined to be unreasonable.)[14]

Internet Portal to Assist Consumers in Identifying Coverage Options

The Secretary, in consultation with the states, is required to establish an Internet portal for the public to easily access affordable and comprehensive coverage options. The Secretary is also required to determine the minimum information available through the portal and develop a standardized format for the presentation of information. The Internet portal, www.healthcare.gov, was launched on July 1, 2010.[15]

The portal is required to provide, at minimum, information on the following coverage options: health plans offered in the private insurance market; Medicaid and the State Children's Health Insurance Program (CHIP); high risk pools; and small group health plans. In order to provide coverage information consistently, the interim final rule establishes a standardized format for presentation of information on the portal, including plan eligibility, availability, premium rates, cost-sharing, and the percentage of total premium revenues spent on medical claims compared to administrative costs.[16]

Prohibition of Lifetime Limits and Restriction of Annual Limits

Prior to ACA, plans were generally able to set lifetime and annual limits—dollar limits on how much the plan would spend for covered health benefits either during the entire period an individual was enrolled in the plan (lifetime limits) or during a plan year (annual limits). However, for plan years beginning on or after September 23, 2010, ACA generally prohibits plans from imposing lifetime limits or "restricted" annual limits on the dollar value of health benefits.[17] The limits apply specifically to essential health benefits (EHB).[18] Until the EHB are defined,[19] the Departments (the Departments of Health and Human Services, Labor, and Treasury) will take into account good faith efforts to comply with a reasonable interpretation of EHB. For this purpose, a plan must apply the definition of EHB consistently. For example, a plan cannot apply a lifetime limit and a restricted annual limit to the same benefit; applying a lifetime limit implies the benefit is not an EHB, while applying a restricted annual limit implies that the benefit is an EHB. Because the lifetime and annual limit requirements are tied to EHBs, health plans are allowed to impose limits on non-EHBs.

Lifetime Limits

Plans are prohibited from establishing lifetime limits on the dollar value of EHB for any participant or beneficiary. Plans will be permitted to place lifetime limits on specific covered benefits that are not EHB, to the extent that such limits are otherwise permitted by federal and state law.

Under the interim final rule, individuals who reached the lifetime limit under a plan prior to the applicability date of the regulations and are otherwise still eligible under the plan must be provided with a notice that the lifetime limit no longer applies.[20] If these individuals are no longer enrolled in the plan, then the regulations provide an enrollment (or reinstatement in the individual market) opportunity for such individuals. Individuals who are eligible for this enrollment opportunity or reinstatement are allowed to enroll in any of the benefit packages that are available to similarly situated individuals upon initial enrollment. For individuals who reached the lifetime limit under a group health plan offered by an employer, the interim final rule does not specify whether both current and former employees are entitled to the enrollment opportunity.

Restricted Annual Limits

Prior to January 1, 2014, plans may establish restricted annual limits on the dollar value of EHB; in 2014 annual limits will be prohibited similar to lifetime limits. The restricted annual limits are phased in over a period of three years. Under this approach, annual limits on the dollar value of benefits may not be less than the following amounts according to plan years:

- for plan years beginning on or after September 23, 2010, but before September 23, 2011: $750,000;
- for plan years beginning on or after September 23, 2011, but before September 23, 2012: $1.25 million; and
- for plan years beginning on or after September 23, 2012, but before January 1, 2014: $2 million.

Plans may use higher annual limits than the amounts listed above or impose no limits before January 1, 2014. The provision for restricted annual limits sunsets with the plan year beginning January 1, 2014, at which time plans will not be allowed to impose any annual limits.

According to ACA, in defining the restricted annual limits the Secretary should "ensure that access to needed services is made available with a minimal impact on premiums."[21] To this end, HHS established a process whereby limited benefit plans could request and HHS could grant waivers from the restrictions on annual limits. Limited benefit plans generally offer coverage with restrictive annual limits on total benefits and/or specific service categories. Regulators assumed that applying the restriction on annual limits to limited benefit plans would result in significant decreases in benefits and/or significant increases in premiums.[22] The waivers are temporary; in 2014 all plans, including limited benefit plans, are prohibited from establishing annual limits on EHB.[23]

Prohibition on Rescissions

The practice of "rescission" refers to the retroactive cancellation of medical coverage after an enrollee has become sick or injured. Effective for plan years beginning on or after September 23, 2010, ACA generally prohibits rescissions. Rescissions will still be permitted in cases where the covered individual committed fraud or made an intentional misrepresentation of material fact as prohibited by the terms of the plan. A cancellation of coverage in this case requires prior notice to the enrollee.

The interim final rule requires a health plan to provide at least 30 calendar days advance notice to an individual before coverage may be rescinded.[24] The rule provides that any state or federal law that applies to a rescission or cancellation of coverage that is more protective of individuals, beyond the standards established by ACA, would apply in place of the ACA provision.

Coverage of Preventive Health Services with No Cost-Sharing

Effective for plan years beginning on or after September 23, 2010, health plans are required to provide coverage for preventive health services without cost-sharing.[25] The preventive services include the following minimum requirements:[26]

- evidence-based items or services that have in effect a rating of "A" or "B" from the United States Preventive Services Task Force (USPSTF);[27]
- immunizations that have in effect a recommendation from the Advisory Committee on Immunization Practices of the Centers for Disease Control and Prevention (CDC);[28]
- evidence-informed preventive care and screenings (for infants, children, and adolescents) provided for in the comprehensive guidelines supported by the Health Resources and Services Administration (HRSA);[29] and

- additional preventive care and screenings for women not described by the USPSTF, as provided in comprehensive guidelines supported by HRSA.[30]

Additional services not recommended by the USPSTF may be offered, but are not required. For the purposes of this provision and others in federal law, ACA negates the November 2009 USPSTF recommendation that women receive routine screening mammograms beginning at age 50. As a result, plans are required to cover screening mammograms beginning at age 40, based on the prior USPSTF recommendation.[31]

ACA permits the Secretary to develop guidelines for plans to utilize value-based insurance designs. Value-based insurance designs refer to coverage that encourages the use of services that have clinical benefits exceeding the costs, while discouraging the use of services when the expected clinical benefits do not justify the costs.[32]

It should be noted that with respect to a plan that has a network of providers, the plan is not required to provide coverage for a recommended preventive service that is delivered by an out-ofnetwork provider, and the plan may impose cost-sharing requirements for a recommended preventive service delivered out-of-network. Additionally, if a recommended preventive service does not specify the frequency, method, treatment, or setting for the service, then the plan can determine coverage limitations by relying on established techniques and relevant evidence.[33]

Extension of Dependent Coverage

Effective for plan years beginning on or after September 23, 2010, ACA requires that if a plan provides for dependent coverage, the plan must make such coverage available to a child under age 26.[34] ACA does not require plans to offer dependent coverage; if a plan chooses not to provide such coverage, nothing in this statute requires them to do so.[35] The age requirement affects only plans that choose to offer dependent coverage. Some specifics of this provision are listed below.

- Plans that *offer* dependent coverage must continue to make that offer available until the adult child turns 26 years of age.
- Plans must make coverage available for both married and unmarried adult children under age 26, but not for the adult child's children or spouse.

- With one exception, these provisions apply to grandfathered plans. Prior to 2014, grandfathered group plans are not required to make dependent coverage available to adult children who can enroll in an eligible employer-sponsored plan based on their employment. (However, if a health plan wishes it may voluntarily make dependent coverage available to children with employer offers of coverage.)[36]

Prohibition of Discrimination Based on Salary

Effective for plan years beginning on or after September 23, 2010, the sponsors of health plans are prohibited from establishing eligibility criteria, for any full-time employee, that are based on the total hourly or annual salary of the employee.[37] In no way will eligibility rules be permitted to discriminate in favor of higher wage employees.

Medical Loss Ratio

Under ACA, health plans are required to submit to the Secretary a report concerning the percent of premium revenue spent on medical claims ("medical loss ratio" or MLR).[38] The ACA MLR calculation includes adjustments for health quality costs, taxes, regulatory fees, and other factors. The law requires plans in the individual and small group markets to meet a minimum MLR of 80%; for large groups, the minimum MLR is 85%.[39] States are permitted to increase the percentages, and the Secretary may adjust the state percentage for the individual market if it is determined that the application of a minimum MLR of 80% would destabilize the individual market within the state.[40]

These reporting requirements are effective beginning in plan year 2011, with the first annual report due to HHS by June 2012 for the prior plan year. Health plans whose MLR falls below the specified limit must provide rebates to policyholders on a pro rata basis. Any required rebates must be paid to policyholders by August of that year.[41]

Appeals Process

Effective for plan years beginning on or after September 23, 2010, the law requires that plans implement an effective appeals process for coverage determinations and claims.[42] The process at a minimum must

- have an internal claims appeals process;
- provide notice to enrollees of available internal and external appeals processes, and the availability of any applicable assistance; and

- allow an enrollee to review their file, present evidence and testimony and to receive continued coverage pending the outcome.

To comply with the requirements for the *internal* claims appeals process, group plans are expected to initially incorporate the claims and appeals procedures previously established under federal law[43] and will update their processes in accordance with any standards established by the Secretary of Labor. Individual health plans will comply with internal claims and appeals procedures set forth under applicable law and updated by the Secretary of HHS.

To comply with the requirements of the *external* review processes, plans must comply with the applicable state external review process that at a minimum includes the consumer protections set forth in the Uniform External Review Model Act promulgated by the National Association of Insurance Commissioners (NAIC).[44] The health plan is required to implement an effective external review process that meets the minimum standards established by the Secretary of HHS, if the applicable state has not established standards that meet the NAIC model requirements, or if the plan is self-insured and therefore not subject to state insurance regulation.[45]

Coverage of Preexisting Health Conditions for Children

ACA prohibits coverage exclusions for children under age 19 with preexisting health conditions, effective for plan years beginning on or after September 23, 2010.[46] A "preexisting health condition" is a medical condition that was present before the date of enrollment for health coverage, whether or not any medical advice, diagnosis, care, or treatment was recommended or received before such date. Excluding coverage for preexisting conditions refers to the circumstance in which an applicant for coverage is offered health insurance but that coverage does not provide benefits for treating the applicant's current medical conditions. The interim final rule broadly defines preexisting conditions to include the outright denial of coverage, as well as the exclusion of specific benefits.[47]

Patient Protections

Effective for plan years beginning on or after September 23, 2010, plans are subject to three ACA requirements relating to the choice of health care professionals and one ACA requirement relating to benefits for emergency services.[48]

Regarding the choice of health care professionals, a plan that requires or allows an enrollee to designate a participating primary care provider is required to permit the designation of any participating primary care provider who is available to accept the individual. This same provision applies to pediatric care for any child who is a plan participant. A plan that provides coverage for obstetrical or gynecological care cannot require authorization or referral by the plan or any person (including a primary care provider) for a female enrollee who seeks obstetrical or gynecological care from an in-network health care professional who specializes in obstetrics or gynecology.

If the plan covers services in an emergency department of a hospital, the plan is required to cover those services without the need for any prior authorization and without the imposition of coverage limitations, irrespective of the provider's contractual status with the plan. If the emergency services are provided out-of-network, the cost-sharing requirement will be the same as the cost-sharing for an in-network provider.

Uniform Explanation of Coverage Documents

The ACA required the Secretaries of HHS, Labor, and Treasury (hereinafter, the Secretaries) to develop standards for plans with respect to providing their enrollees with a summary of benefits and coverage (SBC), no later than March 23, 2011.[49] The Secretaries will periodically review and update the standards developed. The Secretaries will consult with the NAIC; representatives of health-insurance related consumer advocacy organizations; health insurance issuers; health care professionals; patient advocates, including those representing individuals with limited English proficiency; and other qualified individuals as deemed appropriate. These federal standards preempt any standards developed under state law. Table 1 summarizes the standards for the SBC according to ACA.

ACA requires that each plan provide a SBC to individuals at the time of application, prior to the time of enrollment or re-enrollment, and when the insurance policy is issued. The SBC can be in paper or electronic form. Enrollees must be given notice of any material changes in benefits no later than 60 days prior to the date that the modifications would become effective. Any entity that willfully fails to provide the information required is subject to a fine of not more than $1,000 for each such failure, defined as each enrollee that did not receive the required information. ACA also requires that plans provide a uniform glossary of terms commonly used in health insurance coverage (e.g., coinsurance) to enrollees upon request.[50]

ACA requires that plans begin providing the SBC and the uniform glossary no later than March 23, 2012, and the notice of proposed rulemaking (published August 22, 2011)[51] suggests this applicability date. However, after reviewing the comments submitted on this issue, the Secretaries determined that it would not be feasible to require plans to comply with the standards by March 23, 2012. The final rule delays the applicability date of the provision for six months. Generally, plans must comply with the requirements to provide an SBC and the uniform glossary on or after September 23, 2012.[52]

Table 1. Summary of Benefits and Coverage Document Requirements

Issue Area	Requirements
Prohibitions	• Cannot exceed 4 pages in length.
	• Cannot use smaller than 12-point font.
Required description	• Coverage including cost-sharing for each of the essential health benefit categories.
	• Any exceptions, reductions, and limitations on coverage.
	• Renewability and continuation provisions.
	• Whether the plan covers minimum essential benefits.
	• Other benefits as identified by the Secretary.
	• Contact information including a phone number and Internet web address for consumer information.
Other requirements	• Must be presented in a culturally and linguistically appropriate manner utilizing language understandable by the average plan enrollee.
	• Must use uniform definitions of standard insurance and medical terms.
	• Must have a statement ensuring that not less than 60% of allowed costs are covered by the benefits.
	• Must have a statement that the document is a summary and should not be consulted to determine the governing contractual provisions.

Source: CRS analysis of ACA.

Reporting Requirements Regarding Quality of Care

Beginning upon ACA enactment (March 23, 2010) and concluding no later than two years after enactment, the Secretary must develop reporting requirements for use by plans, including regulations governing acceptable provider reimbursement structures.[53] (To date, the Secretary has not published the reporting requirements.) The Secretary must develop these requirements in consultation with experts in health care quality and other stakeholders. Once implemented, plans will annually submit to the Secretary and to enrollees a report addressing whether plan benefits and reimbursement structures do the following:

- improve health outcomes through use of quality reporting, case management, care coordination and chronic disease management;
- implement activities to prevent hospitalization readmissions;
- implement activities to improve patient safety and reduce medical errors through the use of best clinical practices, evidence based medicine, and health information technology; and
- implement wellness and health promotion activities.

The Secretary is required to make these reports available to the public, and is permitted to impose penalties for noncompliance.

Wellness and health promotion activities include personalized wellness and prevention services, and specifically efforts related to smoking cessation, weight management, stress management, physical fitness, nutrition, heart disease prevention, healthy lifestyle support, and diabetes prevention. These services may be made available by entities (for example, health care providers) who conduct health risk assessments or who provide ongoing face-to-face, telephonic, or web-based intervention efforts for program participants.[54]

2014 Market Reforms

In addition to the immediate reforms in ACA, there are additional private insurance market reforms that become effective for plan years beginning on or after January 1, 2014.[55] These reforms include the following:

- nondiscrimination based on health status;
- guaranteed issue and guaranteed renewability;
- coverage of preexisting health conditions (regardless of age);
- nondiscrimination regarding clinical trial participation;
- rating restrictions;
- waiting period limitation; and
- nondiscrimination regarding health care providers.

As in the previous section of this report, it is important to note that the reforms often apply differently to health plans according to the market segment in which the plan is offered and whether the plan has grandfathered status. In the text of this report the term "plan" is used generally; for more specific information as to the specific types of plans (i.e., a grandfathered plan in the large group market) to which the reform applies, see Appendix B.

Nondiscrimination Based on Health Status

ACA prohibits health plans from basing eligibility or coverage on health status-related factors.[56] Such factors include health status, medical condition (including both physical and mental illness), claims experience, receipt of health care, medical history, genetic information, evidence of insurability (including conditions arising out of acts of domestic violence), disability, and any other health status-related factor determined appropriate by the Secretary. ACA allows, however, for the offering of premium discounts or rewards based on enrollee participation in wellness programs, in keeping with prior federal law.[57]

Guaranteed Issue and Guaranteed Renewability

ACA requires coverage to be offered on a guaranteed issue basis, as well as on a guaranteed renewal basis.[58] "Guaranteed issue" in health insurance is the requirement that a plan accept every applicant for health coverage, as long as that applicant agrees to the terms and conditions of the insurance offer (such as the premium). Under ACA, plans are allowed to restrict guaranteed issue coverage to open and special enrollment periods.[59] "Guaranteed renewability" in health insurance is the requirement on a plan to renew individual coverage at the option of the policyholder, or renew group coverage at the option of the plan sponsor (e.g., employer).

Coverage of Preexisting Health Conditions (Regardless of Age)

Beginning in 2014, ACA prohibits plans from excluding coverage for preexisting health conditions, regardless of the age of the covered individual.[60] In other words, plans may not exclude benefits based on health conditions for any individuals. (For persons under age 19, this provision became effective for plan years beginning on or after September 23, 2010.)

Nondiscrimination Regarding Clinical Trial Participation

ACA prohibits health plans from

- prohibiting "qualified individuals" from participating in an approved clinical trial;

- denying, limiting, or placing conditions on the coverage of routine patient costs associated with participation in an approved clinical trial; and
- discriminating against "qualified individuals" on the basis of their participation in approved clinical trials.[61]

ACA defines qualified individual, for purposes of this provision, as an individual who is eligible to participate in an approved clinical trial for treatment of cancer or other life-threatening disease or condition, and who either has a referring health care provider who has concluded that the individual's participation is appropriate, or who provides medical and scientific information establishing that participation in a clinical trial would be appropriate.

Rating Restrictions

ACA imposes adjusted (or modified) community rating rules on the determination of premiums.[62] "Adjusted community rating" rules prohibit health plans from pricing health insurance products based on health factors, but allows it for other key characteristics such as age or gender. ACA's rating rules restrict premium variation to the following factors: self-only or family enrollment; rating area,[63] as specified by the state; age (by no more than a 3 to 1 ratio across age rating bands established by the Secretary, in consultation with the NAIC);[64] and tobacco use (by no more than 1.5 to 1 ratio).[65]

Waiting Period Limitation

ACA prohibits plans from establishing waiting periods greater than 90 days.[66] A "waiting period" refers to the time period that must pass before an individual is eligible to be covered by health benefits.

Nondiscrimination Regarding Health Care Providers

ACA imposes nondiscrimination requirements with respect to health care providers.[67] Plans are not allowed to discriminate, with respect to participation under the plan, against any health care provider who is acting within the scope of that provider's license or certification under applicable state law. This provision does not require a plan to contract with any health care provider willing to abide by the plan's terms and conditions, and the provision cannot be construed as preventing a plan or the Secretary from establishing varying reimbursement rates for providers based on quality or performance measures.

APPENDIX A. STATUS OF REGULATIONS

Health Insurance Market Reform	Status of Federal Regulations	Federal Register Entry	Effective Date of Regulation[a]	Applicability and Date[b]
Rate Review	Final rule: May 23, 2011 by the Department of HHS	76 Federal Register 29964	July 18, 2010	No stated applicability.
	Amendment to final rule: September 6, 2011 by the Department of HHS	76 Federal Register 54969	November 1, 2011	No stated applicability.
	Proposed amendment to final rule: November 26, 2012 by the Department of HHS	77 Federal Register 70584	N.A.	N.A.
Internet Portal to Assist Consumers in Identifying Coverage Options	Interim final rule: May 5, 2010 by the Department of HHS	75 Federal Register 24470	May 10, 2010	No stated applicability.
Prohibition of Lifetime Limits and Restriction of Annual Limits	Interim final rule: June 28, 2010 by the Departments of HHS, Labor, and Treasury	75 Federal Register 37188	August 27, 2010	The interim final rule generally applies to group health plans, group health insurance coverage, and individual health insurance coverage, for plan years and policy years beginning on or after September 23, 2010.
Prohibition on Rescissions	Interim final rule: June 28, 2010 by the Departments of HHS, Labor, and Treasury	75 Federal Register 37188	August 27, 2010	The interim final rule generally applies to group health plans, group health insurance coverage, and individual health insurance coverage, for plan years and policy years beginning on or after September 23, 2010.

(Continued)

Health Insurance Market Reform	Status of Federal Regulations	Federal Register Entry	Effective Date of Regulation[a]	Applicability and Date[b]
Coverage of Preventive Health Services with No Cost-sharing	Interim final rule: July 19, 2010 by the Departments of HHS, Labor, and Treasury	75 Federal Register 41726	September 17, 2010	The interim final rule implements the regulations for coverage of preventive services and generally applies to group health plans, group health insurance issuers, and individual health insurance issuers for plan years and policy years beginning on or after September 23, 2010.
	Amendments to the interim final rule: August 3, 2011 by the Departments of HHS, Labor, and Treasury	76 Federal Register 46621	August 1, 2011	The amendments to the interim final rule outline the ability of the Departments to exempt certain religious employers from providing coverage for contraceptive services. The amendments generally apply to group health plans and group health insurance issuers on August 1, 2011.
	Final rule: February 15, 2012 by the Departments of HHS, Labor, and Treasury	77 Federal Register 8725	April 16, 2012	The final rule finalizes the provisions of the interim final rule relating to the authorization of an exemption of religious employers from having to cover preventive health services relating to contraception. The final rule generally applies to group health plans and group health insurance issuers beginning April 16, 2012.
	Advance Notice of Proposed Rulemaking (ANPRM): March 21, 2012 by the Departments of HHS, Labor, and Treasury	77 Federal Register 16501	No effective date	The ANPRM announces the intention of the Departments to propose amendments to the final rule relating to alternatives for certain religious employers who are required to cover preventive health services relating to contraception. The ANPRM serves as a request for comments, which were due on or before June 19, 2012.

Health Insurance Market Reform	Status of Federal Regulations	Federal Register Entry	Effective Date of Regulation[a]	Applicability and Date[b]
	Proposed Rule: February 6, 2013, by the Departments of HHS, Labor, and Treasury	78 Federal Register 8456	N.A.	N.A.
Extension of Dependent Coverage	Interim final rule: May 13, 2010 by the Departments of HHS, Labor, and Treasury	75 Federal Register 27122	July 12, 2010	The interim final rule generally applies to group health plans, group health insurance issuers, and individual health insurance issuers for plan years and policy years beginning on or after September 23, 2010.
Prohibition of Discrimination Based on Salary	No regulatory action to date			
Medical Loss Ratio (MLR)	Interim final rule: December 1, 2010 by the Department of HHS	75 Federal Register 74864	January 1, 2011	The interim final rule generally applies, beginning January 1, 2011, to health insurance issuers offering group or individual health insurance coverage.
	Final rule: December 7, 2011 by the Department of HHS	76 Federal Register 76574	January 3, 2012	The final rule contains amendments to the interim final rule relating to mini-med plans, among other provisions. The amendments in the final rule generally apply to health insurance issuers offering group or individual health insurance coverage beginning January 1, 2012.
	Amendment to final rule: May 16, 2012 by the Department of HHS	77 Federal Register 28790	June 15, 2012	The amendments establish notice requirements for issuers in the group and nongroup markets that meet or exceed the applicable MLR standard in the 2011 reporting year. The amendments generally apply, beginning July 1, 2012, to issuers offering group and nongroup coverage.

(Continued)

Health Insurance Market Reform	Status of Federal Regulations	Federal Register Entry	Effective Date of Regulation[a]	Applicability and Date[b]
	Proposed Rule: December 7, 2012 by the Department of HHS	77 Federal Register 73118	N.A.	N.A.
Appeals Process	Interim final rule: July 23, 2010 by the Departments of HHS, Labor, and Treasury	75 Federal Register 43330	September 21, 2010	The interim final rule generally applies to group health plans, group health insurance issuers, and individual health insurance issuers for plan years and policy years beginning on or after September 23, 2010.
	Amendment to interim final rule: June 24, 2011 by the Departments of HHS, Labor, and Treasury	76 Federal Register 37208	June 22, 2011	N.A.
Coverage of Preexisting Health Conditions for Children	Interim final rule: June 28, 2010 by the Departments of HHS, Labor, and Treasury	75 Federal Register 37188	August 27, 2010	The interim final rule generally applies to group health plans, group health insurance coverage, and individual health insurance coverage, for plan years and policy years beginning on or after September 23, 2010.
Patient Protections	Interim final rule: June 28, 2010 by the Departments of HHS, Labor, and Treasury	75 Federal Register 37188	August 27, 2010	The interim final rule generally applies to group health plans and group health insurance issuers for plan years beginning on or after September 23, 2010.
Uniform Explanation of Coverage Documents	Final Rule: February 14, 2012 by the Departments of HHS, Labor, and Treasury	77 Federal Register 8668	April 16, 2012	The requirements apply to group health plans beginning on the first day of the first open enrollment period that begins on or after September 23, 2012 (for participants who enroll or re-enroll during an open enrollment period)

Health Insurance Market Reform	Status of Federal Regulations	Federal Register Entry	Effective Date of Regulation[a]	Applicability and Date[b]
				and beginning on the first day of the first plan year that begins on or after September 23, 2012 (for newly eligible individuals). The requirements apply to issuers of coverage in the individual market beginning September 23, 2012.
Reporting Requirements Regarding Quality of Care	No regulatory action to date			
Nondiscrimination Based on Health Status	No regulatory action to date			
Guaranteed Issue and Guaranteed Renewability	Proposed rule: November 26, 2012 by the Department of HHS	77 *Federal Register* 70584	N.A.	N.A.
Coverage of Preexisting Health Conditions (Regardless of Age)	Interim final regulation: June 28, 2010 by the Departments of HHS, Labor, and Treasury	75 *Federal Register* 37188	August 27, 2010	The interim final rule generally applies to group health plans, group health insurance coverage, and individual health insurance coverage for plan years and policy years beginning on or after January 1, 2014.
Nondiscrimination Regarding Clinical Trial Participation	No regulatory action to date			
Rating Restrictions	Proposed rule: November 26, 2012 by the Department of HHS	77 *Federal Register* 70584	N.A.	N.A.
Waiting Period Limitation	No regulatory action to date			
Nondiscrimination Regarding Health Care Providers	No regulatory action to date			

Source: CRS analysis of federal regulations, all available at https://www.federalregister.gov/.

Note: N.A. is used to indicate instances when certain information is not specified in a proposed rule. The table references proposed rules only in cases where a final rule has not yet been published.

[a] The "effective date" of the regulation is the date which the regulation takes effect, as stated in the *Federal Register* notice. The effective date of the regulation is not necessarily the date in which all provisions of the regulation become effective.

[b] "Date" in this context is the date on which the regulation generally applies to affected entities, as stated in the *Federal Register* notice.

APPENDIX B. APPLICABILITY OF MARKET REFORMS TO HEALTH PLANS

Table B-1. Applicability of ACA's Private Health Insurance Market Reforms to Health Plans

	Grandfathered Plans[a]			New Plans (Non-grandfathered)				
	Group Market[b]			Large Group Market[c]		Small Group Market[d]		
Provision	**Fully insured[e]**	**Selfinsured[f]**	**Individual Market[g]**	**Fully insured**	**Selfinsured**	**Fully insured**	**Selfinsured**	**Individual Market**
	"Immediate" Market Reforms							
Rate Review	N.A.	N.A.	NA	N.A.h	N.A.	yes	N.A.	yes
Prohibition on Lifetime Limits	yes	yes	yes	yes	yes	yes	yes	yes
Restricted Annual Limits	yes	yes	NA	yes	yes	yes	yes	yes
Prohibition on Annual Limits	yes	yes	NA	yes	yes	yes	yes	yes
Prohibition on Rescissions	yes	yes	yes	yes	yes	yes	yes	yes
Coverage of Preventive Health Services with No Cost-sharing	N.A.	N.A.	NA	yes	yes	yes	yes	yes
Extension of Dependent Coveragei	yes	yes	yes	yes	yes	yes	yes	yes
Prohibition of Discrimination Based on Salary	N.A.	N.A.	NA	yes	N.A.	yes	N.A.	N.A.
Medical Loss Ratio (MLR)	yes	N.A.	yes	yes	N.A.	yes	N.A.	yes
Appeals Process	N.A.	N.A.	NA	yes	yes	yes	yes	yes
Coverage of Preexisting Health Conditions for Children	yes	yes	NA	yes	yes	yes	yes	yes
Patient Protections	N.A.	N.A.	NA	yes	yes	yes	yes	yes

	Grandfathered Plans[a]			New Plans (Non-grandfathered)				
	Group Market[b]			Large Group Market[c]		Small Group Market[d]		
Provision	**Fully insured[e]**	**Selfinsured[f]**	**Individual Market[g]**	**Fully insured**	**Selfinsured**	**Fully insured**	**Selfinsured**	**Individual Market**
Uniform Explanation of Coverage Documents	yes	yes	yes	yes	yes	yes	yes	yes
Reporting Requirements Regarding Quality of Care	N.A.	N.A.	NA	yes	yes	yes	yes	yes
	2014 Market Reforms							
Nondiscrimination Based on Health Status	N.A.	N.A.	N.A.	yes	yes	yes	yes	yes
Guaranteed Issue & Guaranteed Renewal	N.A.	N.A.	N.A.	Yes	N.A.	yes	N.A.	yes
Coverage of Preexisting Health Conditions (Regardless of Age)	yes	yes	N.A.	yes	yes	yes	yes	yes
Nondiscrimination Regarding Clinical Trial Participation	N.A.	N.A.	N.A.	yes	yes	yes	yes	yes
Rating Restrictions	N.A.	N.A.	N.A.	N.A.j	N.A.	yes	N.A.	yes
Waiting Period Limitation	yes	yes	N.A.	yes	yes	yes	yes	N.A.
Nondiscrimination Regarding Health Care Providers	N.A.	N.A.	N.A.	yes	yes	yes	yes	yes

Source: CRS Analysis of ACA.

Notes: N.A. indicates that the reform is not applicable to that type of health insurance plan. These market reforms do not apply to retiree-only health coverage (see footnote 9). The reform "Internet Portal to Assist Consumers in Identifying Coverage Options" is not included in this table because the reform does not apply to health plans. Student health plans that are self-insured do not fit under any of these health plan types; therefore, self-insured student plans are not subject to ACA's market reforms.

[a] A grandfathered plan refers to an existing group health plan or a health insurance plan/policy in which at least one individual is enrolled since March 23, 2010. To maintain grandfathered status, a plan must avoid certain changes to benefits, cost-sharing, employer contributions, and access to coverage.

[b] Health insurance can be provided to a group of people that are drawn together by an employer or other organization, such as a trade union. Such groups are generally formed for some purpose other than obtaining insurance, like employment. When insurance is provided to a group, it is referred to as “group coverage” or “group insurance.” In the group market, the entity that purchases health insurance on behalf of a group is referred to as the plan “sponsor.”

[c] Prior to ACA, large groups were defined as groups with more than 50 workers. For plan years beginning before January 1, 2016, a state may elect to keep the previous definition of large groups, or change the definition to include those groups with more than 100 workers, applicable to ACA-created exchanges and market reforms. For plan years beginning on or after January 1, 2016, large groups must be defined as groups with more than 100 workers.

[d] Prior to ACA, small groups were defined as groups with 2 to 50 workers, although some states also included self-employed individuals ("groups of one”) in the small group market. For plan years beginning before January 1, 2016, a state may elect to keep the previous definition of small groups, or change the definition to include those groups with 1-100 workers, applicable to ACA-created exchanges and market reforms. For plan years beginning on or after January 1, 2016, small groups must be defined as groups with 1-100 workers.

[e] A fully insured health plan is one in which the plan sponsor purchases health coverage from a state-licensed insurance carrier; the carrier assumes the risk of paying the medical claims of the sponsor’s enrolled members.

[f] Self-insured plans refer to health coverage that is provided directly by the organization seeking coverage for its members (e.g. a firm providing health benefits to its employees). Such organizations set aside funds and pay for health benefits directly. Under self-insurance, the organization bears the risk for covering medical claims.

[g] Consumers who are not associated with a group can obtain health coverage by purchasing it directly from an insurance carrier in the individual (or nongroup) health insurance market.

[h] The final rule regarding rate review specified that this provision would apply only to nongroup and fully insured, small group coverage, and not to large groups.

[i] Prior to 2014, grandfathered group health plans are not required to make dependent coverage available to adult children who can enroll in an eligible employer-sponsored health plan based on their employment; however, if a plan wishes to make dependent coverage available to such adult children it may voluntarily do so.

[j] States have the option to allow issuers of coverage in the large group market to offer plans through an exchange beginning in 2017. If a state permits this, then the rate review provisions will apply to all non-grandfathered, fully insured large group plans in the state (regardless of whether the plan is offered inside or outside an exchange).

End Notes

[1] For simplicity's sake, the term "plan" is used generically in this report. It applies to different types of health coverage provided to groups (e.g., employees of a single firm) and individuals.

[2] While the status of proposed rules is included in Table A-1, information from proposed rules is not summarized in this report.

[3] The reference to group markets technically applies to health plans offered by state-licensed insurance carriers and purchased by employers and other plan sponsors. However, health insurance coverage provided through a group may also be sponsored through "self-insurance." Groups that self-insure set aside funds to pay for health benefits directly, and those groups bear the risk for covering medical expenses generated by the individuals covered under the self-insured plan. For additional information regarding self-insurance, see CRS Report R41069, *Self-Insured Health Insurance Coverage*.

[4] It should be noted that ACA defines "small" differently for various provisions. For more information, see CRS Congressional Distribution Memorandum, "What is Small? Definitions of Small Business in the Patient Protection and Affordable Care Act," by Janemarie Mulvey. The memorandum is available upon request from the memorandum's author.

[5] State regulation of health insurance applies only to state-licensed entities. Since self-insured plans are financed directly by the plan sponsor, such plans are not subject to state law.

[6] Federal regulation applies to both traditional insurance and self-insured plans. For more information about federal regulation of health benefits provided through employment, see CRS Report RS22643, *Regulation of Health Benefits Under ERISA: An Outline*.

[7] Most of the private health insurance provisions amend Title XXVII of the Public Health Service Act (PHSA, 42 U.S.C. 300gg et seq.). Title XXVII includes requirements on health insurance coverage for both the group and nongroup markets, enforcement applicable to such requirements, relevant definitions, and other provisions.

[8] A grandfathered health plan refers to an existing plan in which at least one individual has been enrolled since enactment of ACA (March 23, 2010). To maintain grandfathered status, a plan must avoid certain changes to employer contributions, access to coverage, benefits, and cost-sharing (e.g., any increase in co-insurance requirement). For more information about grandfathered status, see CRS Report R41166, *Grandfathered Health Plans Under the Patient Protection and Affordable Care Act (ACA)*, by Bernadette Fernandez.

[9] The federal exemption for retiree-only health plans is not a new exemption. Retiree-only health plans have been exempt from federal health insurance requirements since enactment of the Health Insurance Portability and Accountability Act of 1996. For additional information about these issues, see CRS Report R41166, *Grandfathered Health Plans Under the Patient Protection and Affordable Care Act (ACA)*, by Bernadette Fernandez.

[10] For example, within one year of enactment of ACA, the Secretary of Health and Human Services is required to develop standards for the summary of benefits and coverage (SBC) that plans are expected to provide to their enrollees (§1001: §2715 PHSA). Plans have to begin offering the standardized SBC within two years of enactment.

[11] §1003.

[12] ACA does not apply the rate review requirements to grandfathered health plans.

[13] For information on state-specific threshold proposals, see http://cciio.cms.gov/programs /marketreforms/rates/ sst.html.

[14] For additional information about the final rule related to rate review under ACA, see CRS Congressional Distribution (CD) memorandum "Final Rule related to Rate Review Provision under PPACA," by Bernadette Fernandez and Mark Newsom, August 1, 2011, available upon request.

[15] ACA required the Internet portal to become available no later than July 1, 2010. The Department of Health and Human Services launched a Spanish-language version of the site on September 8, 2010.

[16] 75 *Federal Register* 24470, May 5, 2010.

[17] §1001: §2711 PHSA.

[18] As defined by §1302(b).

[19] ACA identifies 10 broad benefit categories which must be included in the EHB and instructs the Secretary to further define the EHB. To date, HHS has published a proposed rule (77 *Federal Register* 70644, November 26, 2012) and guidance ("Essential Health Benefits Bulletin," December 16, 2011) related to defining the EHB.

[20] 75 *Federal Register* 37188, June 28, 2010.

[21] §1001: §2711(a)(2) PHSA

[22] For more information about the waiver process for restricted annual limits, see Archived CRS Report R41627, *Waiving the Restriction of Annual Limits in Private Health Insurance* , by Bernadette Fernandez.

[23] A list of all entities that have received waivers is available at http://cciio.cms.gov/resources /files/approved_applications_for_waiver.html.

[24] 75 *Federal Register* 37188, June 28, 2010.

[25] §1001: §2713 PHSA.

[26] The complete list of recommendations and guidelines required to be covered under the regulations is available at http://www.healthcare.gov/news/factsheets/2010/07/preventive-services-list.html.

[27] The USPSTF is currently sponsored by the Agency for Healthcare Research and Quality (AHRQ), as an independent panel of private-sector experts in prevention and primary care issues. For more background see http://www.ahrq.gov/ clinic/uspstfab.htm. A rating of "A" means the preventive service is recommended and there is high certainty that the net benefit is substantial. A rating of "B" means the preventive service is recommended, and there is high certainty that the net benefit is moderate or there is moderate certainty that the net benefit is moderate to substantial. See "U.S. Preventive Services Task Force Grade Definitions" available online at http://www.ahrq.gov/CLINIC/uspstf/ gradespost.htm#brec.

[28] The Advisory Committee on Immunization Practices consists of 15 experts in fields associated with immunization who have been selected by the Secretary of Health and Human Services to provide advice and guidance to the Secretary and the CDC on the control of vaccine-preventable diseases. The Committee develops recommendations for the routine administration of vaccines to children and adults in the civilian population; recommendations include age for vaccine administration, number of doses and dosing interval, and precautions and contraindications. For more information see, http://www.cdc.gov/vaccines/acip/index.html.

[29] HRSA is the primary federal agency within the Department of Health and Human Services for improving access to health care services for people who are uninsured, isolated, or medically vulnerable. HRSA provides leadership and financial support to health care providers in every state and U.S. territory. HRSA grantees provide health care to uninsured people, people living with HIV/AIDS, and pregnant women, mothers and children. For more background see, http://www.hrsa.gov/about/index.html.

[30] HRSA published its guidelines related to women's preventive services in August 2011; the guidelines are found at http://www.hrsa.gov/womensguidelines/. These guidelines include, among other services, coverage for all FDA approved contraceptive methods and sterilization procedures. On February 15, 2012, the Departments of Health and Human Services, Treasury, and Labor (the Departments) issued a final rule that included information regarding the additional preventive care and screenings available to women and their applicability to certain religious employers. On March 21, 2012, the Departments issued an Advance Notice of Proposed Rulemaking with the intention of soliciting comments on proposed amendments to the final rule relating to religious employers and the coverage of contraceptive services. On February 6, 2013, HHS published a proposed rule that would change how certain group health plans and religious employers receive exemptions with respect to the requirement to cover contraceptive services. For more information about the requirement to cover contraceptive services without cost sharing, see CRS Report R42370, *Preventive Health Services Regulations: Religious Institutions' Objections to Contraceptive Coverage*, by Cynthia Brougher.

[31] For more information about the USPTF recommendation for covering mammograms, see the "Coverage of Clinical Preventive Services by Public and Private Insurers" section of CRS Report R41278, *Public Health, Workforce, Quality, and Related Provisions in PPACA: Summary and Timeline*.

[32] Statement of Peter R. Orszag "Health Care and the Budget: Issues and Challenges for Reform" before the Committee on the Budget, United States Senate, June 21, 2007, http://www.cbo.gov/ftpdocs/82xx/doc8255/06-21- HealthCareReform.pdf.

[33] 75 *Federal Register* 41726, July 19, 2010.

[34] The federal requirements provide a minimum requirement. States that already impose requirements beyond attaining age 26 may continue to do so. To the extent that the state law is more restrictive than the federal law, the federal statute would apply.

[35] For more information about the extension of dependent coverage, see CRS Report R41220, *Preexisting Condition Exclusion Provisions for Children and Dependent Coverage under the Patient Protection and Affordable Care Act (ACA)*, by Bernadette Fernandez.

[36] 75 *Federal Register* 27122, May 13, 2010.

[37] §1001: §2716 PHSA.

[38] §1001: §2718 PHSA. For more information about the MLR, see CRS Report R42735, *Medical Loss Ratio Requirements Under the Patient Protection and Affordable Care Act (ACA): Issues for Congress*, by Suzanne M. Kirchhoff and Janemarie Mulvey.

[39] Until 2016, ACA allows states to define the small group market as employers who have up to and including 50 employees or up to and including 100 employees; in 2016 the small group market will be defined as employers who have up to and including 100 employees.

[40] To view a list of state requests for an MLR adjustment, see http://cciio.cms.gov/programs /marketreforms/mlr/statemlr-adj-requests.html.

[41] The list of health insurers owing rebates in 2012 is available at http://cciio.cms.gov/resources /files/mlr-issuerrebates-08052012.pdf.

[42] §1001: §2719 PHSA.

[43] Section 503 of ERISA, codified at 29 CFR §2560.530-1, requires that employee benefit plans provide adequate notice in writing to any participant or beneficiary whose claim for benefits under the plan has been denied, setting forth the specific reasons for such denial, written in a manner calculated to be understood by the participant, and to afford a reasonable opportunity to any participant whose claim for benefits has been denied for a full and fair review by the appropriate named fiduciary of the decision denying the claim.

[44] The NAIC is the organization of insurance regulators for all 50 states, the District of Columbia, and 5 territories. The NAIC is a regulatory support agency that helps state insurance regulators fulfill their obligations to protect the interests of insurance consumers.

[45] State regulation of health insurance applies only to state-licensed entities. Since self-insured plans are financed directly by the plan sponsor, such plans are not subject to state law.

[46] For more information about ACA's prohibition on preexisting condition exclusions for children under age 19, see CRS Report R41220, *Preexisting Condition Exclusion Provisions for Children and Dependent Coverage under the Patient Protection and Affordable Care Act (ACA)*.

[47] 75 *Federal Register* 37188, June 28, 2010.

[48] §1001: §2719A PHSA.

[49] §1001: §2715 PHSA. The Secretaries published a notice of proposed rulemaking regarding standards for the disclosure of a summary of benefits and coverage on August 8, 2011 (76 *Federal Register* 52442).

[50] HHS created the uniform glossary that plans must provide upon request; it is available at http://cciio.cms.gov/ resources/files/Files2/02102012/uniform-glossary-final.pdf.

[51] 76 *Federal Register* 52442, August 22, 2011.

[52] 77 *Federal Register* 8668, February 14, 2012.

[53] §1001: §2717 PHSA. Not later than 180 days after the date on which these regulations are promulgated, the Government Accountability Office (GAO) is required to conduct a study regarding the impact of these activities on the quality and cost of health care, and report its findings to the Senate Committee on Health, Education, Labor, and Pensions, and the House Committee on Energy and Commerce.

[54] With respect to gun rights, a wellness or promotion activity cannot require disclosure or collection of any information in relation to (1) the presence or storage of a lawfully possessed firearm or ammunition in the residence or on the property of an individual, or (2) the lawful use, possession, or storage of a firearm or ammunition by an individual. A health plan issued in accordance with the law is prohibited from increasing premium rates, denying health insurance coverage, and reducing or withholding a discount, rebate, or reward offered for participation in a wellness program on the basis of or on reliance on the lawful ownership, possession, use or storage of a firearm or ammunition.

[55] Unless otherwise noted.

[56] §1201: §2705 PHSA.

[57] The Health Insurance Portability and Accountability Act of 1996 (HIPAA) allows group plans to establish premium discounts or rebates or modify cost-sharing requirements in return for adherence to a wellness program. If a reward is provided based solely on participation in a wellness program, or if it does not provide a reward, the program complies with HIPAA without having to satisfy any additional standards, as long as the program is made available to all similarly situated individuals. If a reward is based on an individual meeting a certain standard relating to a health factor, then the program must meet additional requirements specified in HIPAA regulations. Under ACA, the reward must be capped at 30% of the cost of the employee-only coverage under the plan, but the Secretaries of HHS, Labor, and the Treasury would have the discretion to increase the reward up to 50% of the cost of coverage if the increase is determined to be appropriate.

[58] §1201: §2702, 2703 PHSA.

[59] Plans are required to establish special enrollment periods for qualifying events (as defined in section 603 of the Employee Retirement Income Security Act (ERISA, P.L. 93-406)), and for any events identified in regulations promulgated by the Secretary. To date, the Secretary

has promulgated a proposed rule identifying events that would prompt a special enrollment period (77 *Federal Register*, 70584, November 26, 2012).

[60] §1201: §2704 PHSA.

[61] §1201: §2709 PHSA.

[62] §1201: §2701 PHSA.

[63] For example, some states have enacted rating rules in the individual and small group markets that include geography as a characteristic on which premiums may vary. In these cases, the state has established rating areas. Typically, states use counties or zip codes to define those areas.

[64] "By no more than a 3 to 1 ratio" means that a plan will not be allowed to charge an older individual more than 3 times the premium that the plan will charge a younger individual.

[65] "By no more than a 1.5 to 1 ratio" means that a plan will not be allowed to charge a tobacco user more than 1.5 times the premium that the plan will charge an individual who does not use tobacco.

[66] §1201: §2708 PHSA.

[67] §1201: §2706 PHSA.

In: Private Health Insurance …
Editor: Duke Riggs
ISBN: 978-1-62948-770-0

Chapter 4

THE AFFORDABLE CARE ACT AND SMALL BUSINESS: ECONOMIC ISSUES*

Sean Lowry and Jane G. Gravelle

SUMMARY

The Patient Protection and Affordable Care Act (ACA; P.L. 111-148 and P.L. 111-152) contains several provisions to encourage employer-sponsored health coverage, particularly among small businesses. The provisions that most directly relate to small businesses are (1) an employer penalty for not providing health insurance, (2) a tax credit to increase the affordability of health care for the smallest firms, and (3) small business health insurance exchanges designed to increase plan options and lower plan costs.

Several events have altered ACA's implementation since its enactment in 2010. Most notably, the Obama administration delayed the implementation of the employer penalty and part of the small business health exchanges from 2014 to 2015 to allow for more time for developing these provisions and allowing firms to come into compliance. These delays have added to uncertainty over the potential effects of ACA on small businesses.

First, this report explains how employer-sponsored insurance can be used to address concerns about health insurance coverage and cost. Second, it summarizes the three ACA provisions most relevant to small

---

* This is an edited, reformatted and augmented version of Congressional Research Service, Publication No. R43181, dated August 15, 2013.

businesses, listed above. Next, it analyzes these provisions for their potential effects on small businesses. Last, this report presents several approaches that could address some concerns associated with these provisions (particularly the employer penalty).

According to analysis of the most recent employer size and insurance coverage data, ACA's employer penalty is structured so that it could exempt approximately 96.3% of employer firms simply because they would be too small, and thus fall below the employer penalty threshold of 50 full-time equivalent (FTE) employees. These exempt firms account for approximately 28.1% of all workers. After accounting for firms that already provide insurance, less than 1% of employer firms could be subject to the employer penalty. Although 71.9% of all employees work for firms that are large enough to be potentially subject to the penalty, only about 1.7% of employees work in firms that do not already offer health insurance.

Less than 4% of small businesses that could have been eligible for the small business health care tax credit in 2010 actually claimed it. According to a report by the Government Accountability Office (GAO), many business owners felt that (1) the credit was too small of an incentive to begin offering insurance; (2) even if these small employers offered health insurance, some employees declined coverage because they felt that they cannot afford their share of the premium; and (3) the rules were too complex. President Obama has proposed simplifying and expanding the credit.

Small business health exchanges could help to reduce some barriers to accessing relatively affordable health coverage in the small-group market. By pooling risk among multiple businesses and reducing administrative costs, average insurance costs could reduce costs for these firms. On the other hand, firms with relatively healthier employees could see a rise in insurance costs.

INTRODUCTION

The Patient Protection and Affordable Care Act (ACA; P.L. 111-148 and P.L. 111-152) contains several provisions to encourage employer-sponsored health coverage, particularly among small businesses. The provisions that most directly relate to small businesses are (1) an employer penalty for not providing health insurance, (2) a tax credit to increase the affordability of health care for the smallest firms, and (3) small business health insurance exchanges designed to increase plan options and lower plan costs.

The implementation of the ACA's provisions to encourage employer-sponsored health coverage has been the subject of increasing attention, particularly as they relate to small businesses. The ACA's employer penalty is intended to encourage employers to retain or offer health coverage to their employees.[1] Some maintain that the direct costs of the employer penalty and related compliance costs will be damaging to small businesses.[2] Core issues regarding the employer penalty as related to small businesses include hiring and workforce decisions, as well as their administrative costs. Although the employer penalty may not affect the decisions of employers with few employees (fewer than 50 employees) because they are not subject to the penalty, the penalty could be part of decision-making calculations for employers who are on the margins of the penalty threshold and are considering expanding their business.

Several events have altered ACA's implementation since its enactment in 2010:

- The Supreme Court ruled in 2012 that ACA's requirement that states extend their Medicaid benefits to all adults under the age of 65 with incomes up to the 133% of the federal poverty level was unconstitutional. It is now up to the states to choose whether to expand their respective Medicaid programs and increase health care coverage and affordability among some low-income workers.
- On June 4, 2013, the Department of Health and Human Services (HHS) announced that it is delaying the enforcement of ACA's requirement that the Small Business Health Options Program (SHOP) exchanges offer more than one plan from 2014 to 2015.[3] The SHOP exchanges will still open in 2014, but they are not required to offer more than one plan to employers.
- On July 2, 2013, the Obama Administration announced a delay in implementation of the employer penalty until 2015, citing the need to simplify administrative complexities for businesses and give businesses more time to comply with an appropriate plan.[4] According to the ACA, the employer penalty and the small business health exchanges are supposed to go into effect beginning in 2014.

This report analyzes several ACA provisions that are most relevant to small business.[5] Because there is no single, precise definition of a "small business" in the ACA, this report discusses issues that are relevant to businesses that are sometimes considered to be "small" in more general terms (e.g., fewer than 500 employees). First, an overview of the rationale behind employer-sponsored health insurance is provided. This rationale informs the purpose and design of many of ACA's small-business relevant provisions. Second, a description of the ACA provisions that are most relevant to small business is provided, including the employer penalty, small business health care tax credits, and SHOP exchanges. Third, each provision is analyzed for potential economic effects on small businesses. Lastly, this report presents several approaches that could address some criticisms of ACA's employer penalty, and reduce its effects on small businesses.

THE RATIONALE FOR ENCOURAGING EMPLOYER-SPONSORED HEALTH INSURANCE

From an economic perspective, health insurance and health care markets have fundamental flaws that often lead to an inefficient allocation of resources. This inefficient allocation of resources, also known as a *market failure*, leads to a mismatch between demand and supply for a product because prices fail to accurately reflect the product's costs and benefits. From an economic perspective, the presence of a market failure may provide a justification for government intervention to resolve inefficiencies, unless the cost of correcting the failure is greater than the expected efficiency loss.[6]

Access to health insurance generates *externalities*, or spillover effects to society, that might be difficult for any individual participant in the health insurance market to take into account. For example, more insured individuals decrease the risk that others might contract certain contagious diseases. Also, ill individuals without coverage might use publicly funded resources, especially if their illness becomes serious enough that it depletes their wealth (a negative externality). The net cost of these externalities to society may not be fully reflected, or *internalized*, by firms and workers, in the cost of health insurance. Therefore, the supply and demand for health insurance in the private market may lead to an undesirable level of insurance from the perspective of society as a whole.

In the private market for health care, individuals typically know more about their health status than insurance firms and those that generally desire more health care tend to seek out health insurance. This market failure is called *adverse selection*. Adverse selection makes it difficult for insurance firms to predict costs and establish prices based on predicted costs.[7] Also, individuals who tend to desire the most health care coverage tend to be the least healthy, while healthier people tend to desire less heath care coverage.

Because some healthy people opt to not have health care coverage, the average price of insurance increases, as those now in the insurance pool are less healthy. Rising costs push more people out of the market for health insurance because they believe that the costs of insurance exceed the benefits. The end result is that many individuals, some by choice and some due to cost, will not have health insurance.

In addition, even if both parties are informed about health status, people who have pre-existing conditions or other characteristics that make use of health care more likely (such as old age) may not have, or be able to afford, health insurance.[8] Individuals could be limited in their capacity to pay for health insurance due to low-incomes. In this instance, a lack of individual health care coverage can still impose the same negative spillover effects on society.

Aside from the issues of adverse selection and spillover effects from uninsured individuals, society as a whole can view health insurance not as individual insurance, but as social insurance. From a social insurance perspective, having more insured individuals spreads the risk (and costs) of becoming ill across more individuals including, for example, those born with compromised health, health issues developed during childhood, or those who lose employer health insurance due to a job loss or change in employment.[9]

Various types of risk-pooling mechanisms have been able to reduce the negative externalities associated with the private health care market. The problem of adverse selection and excessive cost has been addressed among the elderly by Medicare and is significantly reduced among the working population by employer-sponsored health insurance (ESI). Some states also limit variations in premium costs. ESI also provides a pooling mechanism that is unrelated to health factors and thus addresses both the adverse selection problem and the problem of being priced out of the market for those with ill health.[10] ESI also tends to reduce administrative costs compared with such costs when individuals purchase coverage on their own. These pooling and administrative advantages are lessened for businesses with few employees.

The price of employer-sponsored health care benefits should, according to economic theory, offset wages so that employees as a group are still incurring the cost of insurance, but do not face the difficulties they would with non-group private insurance purchase. Employers with small pools of individuals may experience some of the same types of problems as individuals. If there is one employee who has (or whose family has) a serious health problem, the cost for insuring the group could be relatively high. Further, administrative costs per employee are larger for small firms; one study estimates these costs are 18% higher for small businesses.[11] Perhaps as a result, large firms are more likely than small firms to offer health care plans and to have higher employee participation rates.

Two crucial elements are cited as necessary to address the problems relating to adverse selection and lack of affordability, especially for those with pre-existing conditions: some form of community pooling so that individuals with health problems (including age) would not have to pay a substantially different price, and a provision to require most individuals to have health insurance. Since 55% of workers (as of 2011) are already covered by insurance provided by an employer (even if not their own, such as their spouse's employer), policies to further encourage ESI could be deemed by some to be desirable.[12] The benefits of ESI could induce more low-risk workers to purchase health insurance, thereby lowering overall risk pools and subsidizing the higher price of insuring workers with comparatively higher risk profiles.

Overview of Provisions Relating to Small Business in the Affordable Care Act

This section briefly describes the provisions in the ACA that are especially relevant to small businesses.[13] A "small business" is defined in multiple ways throughout ACA, and differs from other conventional definitions of a small business. Thus the scope of the firms affected by each provision varies.

Employer Penalty

The ACA sets out a two-part calculation for determining which employers are subject to a monthly imposed penalty for not providing health insurance meeting minimum standards of "affordability" and "adequacy" set forth in the ACA.[14] As previously mentioned, implementation of the employer penalty was originally scheduled to begin in January 2014, but the Obama Administration has delayed the penalty until January 2015.

First, businesses must employ enough workers to qualify as a "large employer" to be subject to the employer penalty. Small businesses with fewer than 50 full-time equivalent (FTE) employees or less are not subject to the penalty.[15] Total FTEs are calculated by adding the total number of "full-time" workers (who average 30 hours per week or more) plus the number of part-time employees aggregated to FTE employees.[16] Seasonal workers are generally not included in determining employer size.

Second, the penalty will only be levied on large employers that have at least one full-time worker that receives a health insurance premium credit in the individual insurance exchange markets that will begin offering coverage in January 2014. Some large employers could have workers that do not purchase insurance through an employer-sponsored plan, thus those employers would not necessarily face a penalty (these scenarios will be discussed in more depth, later in this report).

For employers subject to the penalty, the amount of the penalty depends on whether an employer offers insurance coverage. Even if an employer offers coverage, it could still be subject to the employer penalty if the health insurance coverage does not meet ACA's standards for being *affordable* and *adequate*. Coverage is considered affordable if the employee's required contribution to the plan does not exceed 9.5% of the employee's household income for the taxable year.[17] A health plan is considered to provide adequate coverage if the plan is a 60% or greater actuarial value (i.e., the share of the total allowed costs that the plan is expected to cover).

If a large employer offers coverage that is not *affordable* and *adequate* and one or more of those employees receives premium credits, the monthly penalty is the lesser of

- one-twelfth of $3,000 for each of those employees that receive credits for exchange coverage or
- one-twelfth multiplied by $2,000 multiplied by the number of full-time employees minus 30 (i.e., the first 30 full-time workers are exempted from calculations of the penalty amount).

By comparison, a large employer who does not offer *any* coverage will be subject to a penalty equal to

- the number of its full-time employees minus 30 multiplied by one-twelfth of $2,000 for any applicable month.

Part-time workers are not used to calculate the amount of the employer penalty. After 2014, the penalty payment amount will be indexed by a premium adjustment percentage for each subsequent calendar year. Thus a firm with no more than 30 full-time workers would not pay a penalty even if part-time workers caused them to be classified as "large."

Using 50 employees as the point at which the penalty applies and assuming all full-time employees, a firm with 50 employees, would pay an average monthly penalty of $800 per employee ($2,000 * ((50-30)/50)). The average per employee would rise as employee size rose: $800 per employee for a firm with 50 employees, $909 for 55 employees, $1,000 for 60, $1,200 for 75, $1,400 for 100, $1,880 for 500, and so forth, until the average approaches $2,000 at a very large size.

Small Business Employer Health Care Tax Credit

Small businesses with fewer than 25 FTE employees and with average wages less than $50,000 may be eligible for a credit of up to 50% of the employer's payment for two consecutive years, beginning in 2014.[18] From 2010 through 2013, there is a transitional credit of 35% as well. The employer must pay at least 50% of the health plan premium to be eligible for the tax credit. The tax credit is applied against the income tax, so small employers without tax liability will receive no current benefit and small employers with inadequate tax liability will not receive the full current benefit. Credits can be carried backward one year (except in the first year offered) and forward 20 years.

Tax-exempt entities, such as charities, are eligible for a 35% credit (25% during the transition) taken against payroll taxes.

The credit is phased out both by size and average income in an additive fashion. The credit is reduced by the number of FTE employees over 10, divided by 15; the credit is also reduced by average wage over $25,000 divided by $25,000.

For example, a business with 10 or fewer FTE employees and $25,000 or less in average wages will receive a credit of 50% of the employer contributions to health premiums in 2014.[19] Changes to the size of the firm or its payroll could affect this firm's maximum tax credit in one of three ways:

1. If the average wage remains at $25,000 or less but FTE employee size rises to 15, the credit is reduced by 33% (15 minus 10, all divided by 15, or approximately one-third or 33%).
2. If average wages rise to $30,000 but size mains at 10 or fewer FTE employees, the credit is reduced by 20% ($30,000 minus $25,000, all

divided by $25,000) for a credit of 40% (instead of the maximum of 50%).

3. If both phaseouts are added, so that a firm with 15 employees and an average wage of $30,000, both the 33% and the 20% apply for a reduction of 53%. This combined phaseout would reduce the 50% maximum credit to 23% of employer contributions to health care premiums.

Small Business Insurance Exchanges

Beginning in 2014, small employers seeking health insurance coverage for their employees will be able to use ACA's SHOP exchange.[20] The SHOP exchange is designed to assist small employers and their employees with the purchase of health plans offered in the small group market.[21]

Only qualified small employers and their qualified employees are eligible to obtain coverage through a SHOP exchange health insurance plan. Enrollment in a SHOP exchange begins in October 2013 for the 2014 calendar year. Prior to 2016, states have the option to define "small employers" either as those with 100 or fewer employees or 50 or fewer employees. Beginning in 2016, small employers will be defined as those with 100 or fewer employees.

A SHOP must allow certain "employer choice" functions, thereby enabling an employer to select from a variety of coverage options to make available to its employees. According to an HHS final rule issued on June 4, 2013, however, a SHOP will not be required to carry out the employer choice function (i.e., offer more than one plan) until 2015.[22]

Potential Effects of Certain ACA Provisions on Small Business

This section of the report analyzes the effects certain ACA provisions could have on small businesses. Specifically, issues related to compliance, hiring, and profits are addressed. Although some specific firm size designations are set in the various provisions of the ACA, the effects of these provisions might extend to firms beyond these size thresholds (e.g., those on the margins of growth around the size thresholds).

Employer Penalty

In theory, penalties should help induce firms that are large enough to be subject to the penalty and are not currently providing health insurance to do so, without encouraging other, larger employers to stop providing health insurance. Economic theory suggests the penalty should ultimately be passed through to lower wages, limiting the burden on small business owners.[23] If firms cannot pass on the cost in lower wages, the higher cost of workers may lead firms to reduce output and the number of workers.[24] Individuals with lower incomes, however, should be able to receive insurance premium credits in the community-rated pools, which will increase their welfare while also increasing cost to the federal government for financing coverage to those foregoing ESI. For some firms, paying a penalty may be more feasible than providing insurance that meets ACA's coverage and affordability standards, especially if their employees are lower income and the wage cannot be lowered below the minimum wage.

Any exemption from the employer penalty based on employees could create disincentives for adding workers. As the ACA imposes the full penalty at a specific, discrete level (often referred to as a "cliff"), an additional employee at that point will trigger a significant cost and discourage expansion. By phasing in the penalty as employee size rises, the cost could have risen more gradually and the disincentive at any specific point would be smaller.

The number of small businesses that could be affected by the employer penalty and how they could be affected has been the subject of some misunderstanding among small employers who are not subject to the penalty.[25] A recent survey of very small employers (those with between two to 10 employees) who would not be subject to the employer penalty under ACA found that 56% of respondents misunderstood portions of the ACA's employer penalty, with 32% believing they will be required to provide group health insurance in 2014, regardless of the number of employees, and 24% believe they will have to pay a penalty for failing to provide group coverage.[26]

Data from the Census Bureau's 2010 Statistics of U.S. Business (SUSB) can be used to approximate the number of firms exempt from the employer penalty because they do not have enough employees to put them over the threshold. These data also include information on payroll and wages that are useful for analysis of ACA employer penalties. There are limitations when using SUSB data to analyze ACA penalties. Specifically, full-time and part-time employees count equally as employees in the SUSB dataset, whereas they are weighed differently in calculations of FTE employees. Thus, estimates based on SUSB of the number and share of firms that could be affected by ACA employer penalties are likely overstated. Because the SUSB data does not disaggregate workers by full-time or part-time status, it is also difficult to determine precisely which firms will be "exempt" from the penalty because they have 20 or fewer full-time workers.

Data from the SUSB suggests that the vast majority of firms will be exempt from the employer penalty simply due to their employment size. As shown in **Table 1**, 96.3% of employer firms in 2010 had fewer than 50 employees and thus are not likely to be affected by the ACA employer penalty simply due to their size.[27] These businesses accounted for 28.1% of all workers.

Table 1. Employment and Payroll Characteristics of Employer Firms, 2010

Enterprise Employment Size	Number of Employer Firms	Cumulative Share of All Firms	Average Annual Payroll Per Employer Firm	Number of Employees	Cumulative Share of All Employees	Average Annual Salary Per Employee
45-49	26,529	96.3%	$1,841,331	1,242,981	28.1%	$39,300
50-74	76,223	97.6%	$2,372,354	4,582,829	32.2%	$39,458
75-99	35,946	98.3%	$3,521,044	3,075,081	34.9%	$41,159
100-149	35,590	98.9%	$4,886,593	4,312,353	38.8%	$40,329
150-199	18,195	99.2%	$6,964,260	3,139,298	41.6%	$40,364
200-299	16,184	99.5%	$10,236,390	3,914,153	45.1%	$42,325
300-399	7,449	99.6%	$15,291,626	2,567,426	47.4%	$44,366
400-499	4,355	99.7%	$19,619,523	1,935,310	49.1%	$44,150
500+	17,236	100.0%	$164,449,428	59,973,415	100.0%	$49,750
Total	5,734,538	100.0%	$861,618	111,970,095	100.0%	$44,128

Source: CRS analysis of U.S. Census Bureau, Statistics of U.S. Business Annual Data for 2010, http://www2.census.gov/econ/susb/data/2010/us_naicssector_small_emplsize_2010.xls.

Note: An enterprise is an employment or a business consisting of one or more domestic establishments that were specified under common ownership or control. The enterprise and the establishment are the same for single establishment firms. Each multi-establishment company forms one enterprise. Employment is defined as paid employment and consists of full and part-time employees, including salaried officers and executives of corporations, who were on the payroll in the pay period including March 12. Employment is measured in March, thus some employer firms (e.g., start-ups created after March, closures before March, and seasonal firms) will have zero employment and some annual payroll.

The 3.7% of businesses with 50 or more employees in 2010 which could be potentially subject to the employer penalty (simply based on their size) employed 71.9% of all workers.

When accounting for health insurance offer rates, the number of smaller firms that could be subject to the employer penalty decreases, as the larger the firm, the more likely it is to offer health insurance coverage.[28] Table 2 shows data on health insurance offer rates by firm size from the Kaiser Family Foundation's 2012 Annual Employer Survey.[29] Firms with between three and nine employees were less likely to offer insurance coverage than firms with more employees.[30] In 2012, 87% of firms with fewer than 50 workers offered health benefits to their employees compared to 94% of firms with 50-199 workers, and 98% of firms with 200 workers or more.

Table 2. Percentage of Firms Offering Health Benefits, by Firm Size, 2012

Year	3-9 Workers	10-24 Workers	25-49 Workers	50-199 Workers	200+ Workers
2012	50%	73%	87%	94%	98%

Source: Kaiser Family Foundation (KFF), *Employer Health Benefits Annual Survey*, 2012, p.34, http://ehbs.kff.org/ pdf/2012/8345.pdf.

Note: The KFF survey does not report data for firms with 1-2 workers.

Assuming that the firms offering health care benefits in 2012 continue to do so after the penalty begins in 2014, approximately 0.2% of all employer firms could be subject to the full employer penalty (assuming the coverage provided by employers meet ACA's standards for being "affordable" and "adequate"), with the vast majority of these firms having between 50 and 199 employees.[31] Although the firms with more than 50 employees account for 79.1% of all employees (as shown in Table 1), only about 1.7% of all employees work in larger firms that do not already offer health insurance.[32] Note though, that some analysts' simulations indicate that ACA will have an effect on small business health care coverage rates.[33]

Small Business Employer Health Care Tax Credit

The credit is intended to encourage coverage to benefit very small firms (not subject to the employer penalty) and very low-income workers. The Joint Committee on Taxation (JCT) and the Congressional Budget Office (CBO) initially estimated that taxpayers would claim up to $2 billion in credits for the 2010 tax year.[34] Despite informing approximately 4.4 million taxpayers that were potentially eligible for credits, the Internal Revenue Service (IRS) reported that 228,000 taxpayers claimed the credit for a total of $278 million in 2010.[35] A 2012 report by the Government Accountability Office (GAO) said that the number of firms that benefited from the credit was even smaller than the IRS's 2011 report: 170,300 small businesses claimed a total of $468 million in health care credits in 2010.[36] According to GAO, the average tax credit claimed by small businesses that applied for and received the health care credit in 2010 was $2,748.

GAO found that the amount of small businesses that applied for the credit was limited by three factors. First, many business owners felt that the credit was too small of an incentive to begin offering insurance. Most small businesses that would otherwise be eligible for the credit (83% by one estimate) did not offer health insurance.[37] In addition, 67% of employers who could be eligible for the partial credit did not offer insurance in 2010.[38] Second, even if these small employers offered health insurance, some employees declined coverage because they felt that they could not afford their share of the premium. Third, many small businesses felt that claiming the credit was too complex.[39]

Small Business Insurance Exchanges

The health exchanges associated with ACA, notably the SHOP exchanges, are intended to address some of the inherent disadvantages for small businesses to improve access to affordable health care plans.[40] The 2012 Kaiser Family Foundation Annual Employer Survey reported that among small firms (defined as having 3 to 199 workers) not offering health benefits, 48% cited high cost as "the most important reason" for not doing so.[41] If the ACA programs (including SHOP exchanges) contain the costs of health insurance premiums, more of the smaller firms could offer health insurance coverage.

As with individuals, very small firms that have individuals or families whose health care is relatively more costly will be able to purchase insurance more easily through the SHOP exchanges. For some small firms, the ability to buy insurance through the SHOP exchanges could enable them to offer health coverage at a lower cost than they would have been offered in the private small-group market. This is particularly the case for small businesses that employ workers with a higher risk profile. The cost of these plans are lower because the additional costs of insuring relatively riskier firms will be spread across many other firms. Thus, they should reduce the problem of adverse selection.[42] Firms with healthier employees, however, could see a rise in cost. In any case, the SHOP exchange should also reduce premium costs because of reduced administrative costs from pooling more businesses under a single policy.

POTENTIAL REVISIONS TO ADDRESS CRITICISMS OF THE EMPLOYER PENALTY

Aside from concerns about compliance and administration, some have charged that the employer penalty creates incentives for some employers to take undesirable actions. Some of these possible actions include encouraging firms to avoid hiring or to reduce employment to fall below the limit, significantly increasing the cost of hiring low wage workers, and encouraging firms to reduce the hours of employees to schedule them to work part-time.[43]

Still, an argument could be made that there is no need to make revisions given the small share of firms that would be affected. As noted earlier, the circumstances in which these effects are likely to occur are limited to less than 1% of firms (after adjusting for firms that already offer health insurance coverage). One forecaster has observed that projected employment effects leading up to implementation have not been very large, which may reflect the limited effect of the penalty.[44]

Also, options to liberalize exemptions will increase federal budgetary costs due to lost revenue from the penalty. According to CBO, the employer penalty is expected to raise about $130 billion over 10 years (after accounting for the Obama administration's one-year implementation delay).[45] In addition, if the exemption caused firms to forego offering health insurance, government outlays for health insurance premium credits for individuals would likely increase. This effect would be offset by a reduced cost (i.e., increased revenue), at least in part, from the tax exclusion of health insurance from the income of the employer.

Nevertheless, some may still feel inclined to make revisions to the employer penalty in order to reduce or moderate potential issues. This section of the report analyzes several possible revisions and provides some examples of legislation proposed in the 113th Congress, but it is not meant to reflect an exhaustive list of possible options or suggest that changes are needed.

Eliminate the Employer Penalty

Opposition to the employer penalty is most often centered on its disincentives to hiring on the margins, other possible labor market distortions (e.g., firms choosing to hire part-time to full-time workers), and compliance costs to employers. Some critics have called for a repeal of the current employer penalty, in favor of a complete replacement.[46] In contrast, some bills in the 113th Congress seek to eliminate the employer penalty with no replacement provision that would penalize firms for not offering health insurance of a particular quality or cost level.[47]

As previously mentioned, the employer penalty is designed to encourage employers to either begin offering health insurance to their employees or to maintain coverage.[48] For employers that already offer coverage, the employer penalty serves to reinforce that practice and provide disincentives for firms to decrease the range of coverage or to increase an employee's share of the premium costs.

Change the Definition of "Full-Time" to 40 Hours Per Week

Some have proposed that ACA's definition of a full-time worker be changed to include someone who works 40 hours per week (instead of 30 hours per week). Proponents of this revision argue that the current, 30 hour per week definition is unusually low compared to "traditional standards" of a full-time worker in many industries, thus increasing employer's calculations and compliance costs.[49] In addition, proponents of the revision argue that the 30 hour definition encourages employers to reduce the number of hours allotted to each worker (thereby reducing their pay) in order to reduce the number of "full-time" workers and reduce their compliance costs with ACA (or the size of their employer penalty, since the penalty is only based on full-time workers).[50] Note, as discussed below, that the incentive for firms paying the penalty could be eliminated by imposing the penalty to apply to FTEs.

Several employer surveys indicate that most respondents are not reducing their employees' hours in response to ACA's definition of a full-time worker. According to a 2013 survey conducted by the International Foundation of

Employee Benefits Plans, a non-profit foundation, 16% of the 966 employers surveyed said they have adjusted or plan to adjust hours so that fewer employees qualify for full-time.[51] According to a 2012 survey of 1,203 employers conducted by Mercer, a global business consulting firm, 68% of survey respondents indicated that they will begin offering health coverage to all employees working 30 or more hours per week.[52] Other surveys with fewer respondents support these findings.[53]

In addition to surveys (which could or could not be representative of the firms that could be affected by the employer penalty), some researchers have conducted empirical analysis of broad, public-use data. A 2013 study conducted by the U.C. Berkeley Labor Center estimated that approximately 2.3 million workers in firms with 100 or more employees (representing 3.1% of all workers) were most vulnerable to a reduction in their payroll hours from above 30 hours per week to below 30 hours per week.[54] These workers were mostly concentrated in the restaurant industry. In contrast, a 2013 study conducted by Helen Jorgensen and Dean Baker of the Center for Economic and Policy Research (CEPR) found that less than 1% of all workers in 2013 fall just below ACA's full-time threshold (26-29 hours per week).[55] Jorgensen and Baker's study uses more recent data and is probably a more reliable study to forecast future conditions. Unlike the U.C. Berkeley Labor Center's study, Jorgensen and Baker's study likely captured any initial employers' responses to shifting workers below the 30 hour per week cutoff because, according to ACA, the baseline measurement period for measuring a firm's FTE employees begins in 2013. Also, Jorgensen and Baker's study better captures more recent improvements in the labor market; there are likely to be more "underemployed" workers (working under 40 hours) in the older data because the macroeconomy was in an earlier stage of recovery.

Changing the cutoff from 30 hours per week to 40 hours per week would not eliminate the incentive for employers to shift more workers to part-time status, and could actually provide a greater incentive for firms not to offer health insurance to their employees. In theory, changing the definition of a full-time worker to 40 hours per week would shift, not eliminate, the incentive for employers to reduce workers' hours. Additionally, more employers could be inclined to shift more workers to "part-time" status (in terms of the ACA) under a 40-hour definition, since the disruption to their workforce is smaller from 40 to 39 hours than 40 to 29 hours. If the incentive to retain their workers on full-time status is diminished, then fewer firms could be compelled by the employer penalty to offer health care coverage relative to current law.

Exempt More Firms with Low-Income Employees

Some are concerned that the effects of the employer penalty could be concentrated among smaller firms in certain industries that are large enough to be over the 50-FTE threshold and that primarily employ low-income workers (who are less likely to be able to afford out-of-pocket premium costs of an employer-sponsored health plan). Low-income workers tend to be liquidity constrained in their household budgets. Faced with reducing their take-home paycheck to obtain health insurance coverage, many low-income workers would likely prefer wages to benefits.[56] With the option to receive a government subsidy for health care premiums, an increasing number of lower-income workers could look to the individual exchanges (beginning in 2014) if their employer does not offer affordable coverage. In some cases, this could trigger a penalty for their employer.

The extent to which the interactions between low-income workers and the employer penalty pose a problem to small businesses is unclear at this time. So far, many of these concerns have been voiced by some industry groups (e.g., the restaurant industry). The age of the workers in these industries could have a large effect on whether or not low-income workers will lead to a higher likelihood of their employer's paying the ACA penalty. According to the Bureau of Labor Statistics, the median ages of workers in these industries are over 26.[57] If so, then many of the workers in these industries would not be eligible for extension of dependent coverage. However, some of the workers in these industries, such as food service or retail, could be young enough to be covered as a dependent in a family group plan, covered through an expansion of Medicaid in certain states, or they could find it cheaper to pay the individual penalty than regular health insurance premiums—all of which would not trigger the employer penalty. According to testimony by the National Restaurant Association, 43% of employees are under age 26 in the industry.[58] Media reports indicate that previous estimates of the cost of compliance with the employer penalty among some industries (particularly the restaurant industry) have been revised downward in light of more recent analysis of ACA.[59]

To help increase insurance coverage among lower-income workers, ACA includes an option for states to expand Medicaid to households with incomes up to 133% of the Federal Poverty Line (FPL).[60] As shown in Table 3, this would include families with household income (defined as modified adjusted gross income, or MAGI) up to $15,282 for an individual to $36,668 for a family of five (in 2013).

Table 3. Annual Income by 2013 Federal Poverty Level and Family Size (for the 48 contiguous states and the District of Columbia)

Federal Poverty	Family Size				
Line (FPL)	1	2	3	4	5
100%	$11,490	$15,510	$19,530	$23,550	$27,570
133%	$15,282	$20,628	$25,975	$31,322	$36,668
150%	$17,235	$23,265	$29,295	$35,325	$41,355
200%	$22,980	$31,020	$39,060	$47,100	$55,140

Source: CRS computation based on "Annual Update of the HHS Poverty Guidelines," 78 *Federal Register* 5182, January 24, 2013, http://www.gpo.gov/fdsys/pkg/FR-2013-01-24/pdf/2013-01422.pdf.

Notes: Under ACA, premium credits for eligible exchange coverage will not be available until 2014; the data in this table illustrate the income levels that would apply if premium credits were available in 2013. Different income levels, as measured against the FPL, apply separately to Alaska and Hawaii (see "Annual Update of the HHS Poverty Guidelines" referenced under Source). The poverty guidelines are updated annually for inflation. For space considerations, this chart was limited to households with five people, but the FPL can be calculated for larger households.

However, not all states are expected to expand Medicaid.[61] For those who do not expand, those workers with household income between 100% and 133% of the FPL would be eligible for premium credits in the exchange.[62]

Firms with workers just above the FPL have several options, particularly in those states that do not plan to expand Medicaid. Some employers could find other alternatives to minimize any costs of compliance with the ACA or minimize the size of the penalty that they would face. Even if an employer is limited by ACA in its ability to adjust the scope of coverage and insurance cost-sharing, some could limit more general forms of labor costs. Examples of these options could include reducing the number of current or new hires (or shifting to more capital-intensive modes of production, if possible), reducing the hours allotted to each worker (e.g., moving some workers from full-time to part-time status), or reducing its workers' wages.[63] Reducing the number of employees as well as reducing the average hours worked per employee could have an effect on an employer's potential ACA penalty. Anecdotal media reports indicate that some businesses could provide a low-cost, health plan that does not meet ACA's coverage as a means to reduce the severity of their employer penalty (i.e., pay the reduced penalty rather than the full penalty).[64]

However, the options for employers to pass these costs onto low-income workers are limited in two ways. First, downward pressure on wages is limited in two respects: the minimum wage provides a floor for wages (particularly in industries that require fewer advanced skills), and lower income reduces a firm's ability to attract the best workers (which could become a larger concern as the economy grows).[65] As a result, small employers with low-income employees are less likely to voluntarily offer health insurance coverage as compared to large employers with low-income employees (see Table 3). Second, ACA limits the extent that businesses could require their workers to "pay" for a larger share of employee health benefits. Specifically, the criteria for *affordability* under the ACA limit the amount that workers pay in premiums to 9.5% of their household income (approximately $2,272 for a full-time worker earning minimum wage).[66]

If insurance coverage for low-income workers still remains a concern, then the employer penalty could be modified. Possible modifications include an alternative payroll size exemption and a higher exemption for employers in certain industries.

Create an Alternative Payroll Size Exemption

A dollar-level exemption as an option could exempt more firms with low-income employees where it is more difficult to pass on the costs. One example is the food service industry, whose workers often earn their income in the form of tips rather than wages. Given these claims, an additional exemption could be established based on total firm payroll (either in general or for firms within specific industries) to target these smaller firms.

For example, a $2 million payroll cap could provide an exemption to certain firms, with lower average wages, that would otherwise be subject to ACA employer penalties (because they have too many employees to be exempt).[67] Table 4 provides data on the number of firms in certain industries that have an average payroll of under $2 million but are large enough to be potentially subject to the employer penalty.[68] A full-time worker earning the federal minimum wage would make a gross salary of approximately $15,080.[69] A dollar-level exemption for firms with total payrolls less than $2 million would apply to firms that hired roughly 132 workers at minimum wage ($2 million/$15,080).

Table 4. Illustration of Firms that Could Be Eligible for an Additional $2 Million Payroll Exclusion for Employer Penalties Under the Affordable Care Act

Employee Size Range	Number of Employer Firms	Industry	Total Employment	Average Worker Salary
50-74	135	Agriculture, Forestry, Fishing, and Hunting	7,725	$34,810
50-74	7,456	Retail Trade	418,879	$33,272
50-74	4,775	Administrative and Support and Waste Management and Remediation Services	276,494	$33,685
50-74	2,688	Educational Services	159,433	$29,147
50-74	2,187	Arts, Entertainment, and Recreation	128,352	$22,119
75-99	1,118	Arts, Entertainment, and Recreation	91,369	$24,033
50-74	12,376	Accommodation and Food Services	721,714	$15,529
75-99	4,542	Accommodation and Food Services	371,913	$16,215
100-149	3,665	Accommodation and Food Services	420,057	$15,752
50-74	5,158	Other Services (Except Public Administration)	294,505	$27,244
Total	36,651	All Eligible Industries	2,890,441	$25,181

Source: CRS analysis based on U.S. Census Bureau, Statistics of U.S. Business Annual Data for 2010, http://www2.census.gov/econ/susb/data/2010/us_naicssector_small_emplsize_2010.xls.

Notes: Estimates reflects the number of firms that could be exempt from employer penalties under the Affordable Care Act (ACA) under a policy of a $2 million payroll cap, based on the average payroll size of firms within a particular industry. Because ACA employer penalties are not scheduled to take effect into 2014, the number of firms and employees that could be affected by this option may vary. These calculations do not take into effect current coverage rates among firms in the above industries, thus the actual amount of firms that could be exempted would likely be lower. The $2 million cap is simply an illustration.

Most, *but not all*, of the workers in employer firms that could be exempt under the $2 million cap have a lower average salary than larger firms within their industry. Also, some of these workers have an average salary above 133% of the FPL (as defined in Table 3). Although this is just one possible variation of this policy, these estimates illustrate that an efficient payroll-based exclusion might be easier to design in theory rather than in practice.

As previously mentioned, some workers in the industries in Table 4 might not seek a premium credit in the insurance exchanges for various reasons. More information could be necessary given the limitations of Census data for the purposes of analyzing ACA's employer penalty.

Increase Exemption Limits for Certain Industries

This option would set limits by industry and allow higher FTE-equivalent limits or payroll amounts in certain industries, such as the restaurant industry. Estimates to inform dollar-based exclusions by industry could be conducted to target firms that are below a specific employee-size threshold or below a specific firm payroll or average employee salary.[70]

This option could be more administratively complicated for some firms that, arguably, fall into multiple industry categories. For example, if restaurants were given beneficial treatment, would a doughnut shop that sold for take-away but also served customers at tables be included? Would a micro-brewery with an attached restaurant be included? Similar administrative complications have been encountered with the production activities business tax deduction, which only applies to some industries.[71] For example, an expanded exemption could be based on the North American Industry Classification System (NAICS), as reported on tax filings with business income.[72]

Increase the Exemption for the Employer Penalty to the First 50 Full-Time Workers

Currently, the ACA employer penalty is triggered by the hiring of the 50th FTE worker but the first 30 full-time workers (30+ hours per week) are exempt from the calculation of the penalty size. In other words, a firm that employed 49 full-time workers and then hired a 50th full-time worker would be subject to a penalty based (in part) on 30 full-time workers. This 30 worker exemption could be increased to reduce the "cliff" that firms could face at the hiring of their 50th FTE worker, thereby reducing the marginal disincentive to hire around the employer penalty threshold.

On the other hand, reducing the sheerness of this "cliff" could reduce the marginal incentive that an employer has to begin offering health care to its employees. If fewer firms offer employer-sponsored health plans, then more workers could rely on government subsidies for coverage in individual insurance exchanges.

This option could also reduce the revenue raised by the employer penalty. These revenue losses could be offset, at least in part, by changing the calculation of the penalty from "full-time" workers to "FTE employees" as discussed below. The latter definition would change the calculation of the penalty to include uninsured part-time workers. Although this change might impose a larger compliance burden on some firms, it would also eliminate the incentive for firms to hire part-time workers instead of full-time workers (or reduce the hours of existing full-time workers) in an attempt to reduce their exposure to the employer penalty.

This rule could also be applied if an option based on payroll size were included to eliminate that cliff as well.

Modify the Exemption to the First 30 FTE Employees in Calculating the Penalty

The employer penalty exemption could be revised such that it was based on FTE employees in order to reduce the incentive for firms to hire more part-time workers or change full-time workers to part-time status. In this case, hiring two part time workers to substitute for one full time worker would not change the calculation of the penalty.

This option could be combined with the exemption increase option, below, to offset for at least some of the revenue loss associated with increasing the exemption. For example, the employer penalty could be revised to exempt the first 50 FTE employees, instead of the current exemption of the first 30 full-time employees.

Expand the Small Business Health Care Tax Credit

Although not directly related to the employer penalty, the current small business health care tax credit could be expanded to encourage more small businesses to offer health care coverage (and potentially avoid the employer penalty).

The Obama Administration and some lawmakers have proposed to amend the small business tax credit to encourage and expand its use to more businesses. President Obama's FY2014 budget proposes expanding and simplifying the credit. The budget recommends increasing the eligibility cut-off from 25 to 50 workers, changing the phase-out formula so more firms will qualify for at least part of the credit, and simplifying the calculation of the credit (by removing a requirement that an eligible employer pay a uniform percentage of the premium for each employee and also eliminating a cap on the credit based on the average health insurance premium in the employer's state).[73] The Department of Treasury estimated that this provision would reduce revenue $10.5 billion between FY2014 and FY2023.[74]

In the 113th Congress, the Small Business Health Care Tax Credit Improvement Act of 2013 (H.R. 3046) would amend the tax credit to increase the maximum number of FTEs from 25 to 50, modify the phaseout of the credit, and repeal the limitation based on state health insurance premium averages. Specifically, H.R. 3046 would increase the allowable average annual salaries paid to employees from $25,000 to $28,500 to claim the full credit. Although a cap of $28,500 on average wages would fall below the lower bound average worker wages for all firms with 45 to 49 employees (see Table 1), firms in certain industries listed in Table 4 might be eligible (e.g., arts and entertainment, accommodation and food service). In contrast, the Small Business Tax Credits Improvement Act (S. 1325) would also increase the maximum number of FTEs to 50, increase the maximum wages cap to $37,500, among other provisions to increase the number of firms that could be eligible for the credit and the possible benefits awarded. None of these bills have been reported out of committee as of the date of publication of this report.

APPENDIX. EMPLOYMENT AND PAYROLL CHARACTERISTICS OF EMPLOYER FIRMS, 2010

Table A-1. Employment and Payroll Characteristics of Employer Firms, 2010

Enterprise Employment Size	Number of Employer Firms	Cumulative Share of All Firms	Average Annual Payroll Per Employer Firm	Number of Employees	Cumulative Share of All Employees	Average Annual Salary Per Employee
0-4	3,575,240	62.3%	$63,364	5,926,452	5.3%	$38,225
5-9	968,075	79.2%	$219,032	6,358,931	11.0%	$33,345
10-14	407,404	86.3%	$395,390	4,767,288	15.2%	$33,789
15-19	209,685	90.0%	$582,602	3,521,097	18.4%	$34,695
20-24	120,787	92.1%	$799,265	2,635,563	20.7%	$36,630
25-29	80,526	93.5%	$1,003,321	2,161,156	22.7%	$37,384
30-34	58,557	94.5%	$1,200,384	1,865,736	24.3%	$37,675
35-39	42,860	95.3%	$1,411,879	1,580,717	25.7%	$38,282
40-44	33,697	95.9%	$1,622,666	1,410,309	27.0%	$38,771
45-49	26,529	96.3%	$1,841,331	1,242,981	28.1%	$39,300
50-74	76,223	97.6%	$2,372,354	4,582,829	32.2%	$39,458

Table A-1. (Continued)

Enterprise Employment Size	Number of Employer Firms	Cumulative Share of All Firms	Average Annual Payroll Per Employer Firm	Number of Employees	Cumulative Share of All Employees	Average Annual Salary Per Employee
75-99	35,946	98.3%	$3,521,044	3,075,081	34.9%	$41,159
100-149	35,590	98.9%	$4,886,593	4,312,353	38.8%	$40,329
150-199	18,195	99.2%	$6,964,260	3,139,298	41.6%	$40,364
200-299	16,184	99.5%	$10,236,390	3,914,153	45.1%	$42,325
300-399	7,449	99.6%	$15,291,626	2,567,426	47.4%	$44,366
400-499	4,355	99.7%	$19,619,523	1,935,310	49.1%	$44,150
500+	17,236	100.0%	$164,449,428	59,973,415	100.0%	$49,750
Total	5,734,538	100.0%	$861,618	111,970,095	100.0%	$44,128

Source: CRS analysis of U.S. Census Bureau, Statistics of U.S. Business Annual Data for 2010, http://www2.census.gov/econ/susb/data/2010/us_naicssector_small_emplsize_2010.xls.

Notes: An enterprise is an employment or a business consisting of one or more domestic establishments that were specified under common ownership or control. The enterprise and the establishment are the same for single establishment firms. Each multi-establishment company forms one enterprise. Employment is defined as paid employment and consists of full and part-time employees, including salaried officers and executives of corporations, who were on the payroll in the pay period including March 12. Employment is measured in March, thus some employer firms (e.g., start-ups created after March, closures before March, and seasonal firms) will have zero employment and some annual payroll.

End Notes

[1] For an analysis of other options to increase health insurance coverage (including some that are part of the ACA), see Jonathan Gruber, *Covering the Uninsured in the U.S.*, National Bureau of Economic Research (NBER), Working Paper 13758, January 2008, http://www.nber.org/papers/w13758.pdf.

[2] This concern derives, in part, from the notion that small businesses are critical to job creation. Recent empirical studies indicate that small business owners have different aspirations concerning the growth of their firm, and small, new firms (i.e., startups) are more likely to expand than small businesses, generally. For further information reviewing the theoretical arguments and empirical literature on small business and job creation, see CRS Report R41392, *Small Business and the Expiration of the 2001 Tax Rate Reductions: Economic Issues*, by Jane G. Gravelle and Sean Lowry; CRS Report RL32254, *Small Business Tax Benefits: Current Law and Main Arguments For and Against Them*, by Gary Guenther; and CRS Report R41523, *Small Business Administration and Job Creation*, by Robert Jay Dilger.

[3] See CRS Report R42663, *Health Insurance Exchanges Under the Patient Protection and Affordable Care Act (ACA)*, by Bernadette Fernandez and Annie L. Mach.

[4] See Valerie Jarrett, "We're Listening to Businesses About the Health Care Law," White House Blog, July 2, 2013, http://www.whitehouse.gov/blog/2013/07/02/we-re-listening-businesses-about-health-care-law. For more information about the administrative effects of the delay, see CRS Report R43150, *Delay in Implementation of Potential Employer Penalties Under ACA*, by Bernadette Fernandez and Annie L. Mach.

[5] This report updates and supersedes analysis in the archived CRS Report R40775, *Health Care Reform and Small Business*, by Jane G. Gravelle. For analysis and historical context the alternative proposals put forward during the legislative process that led to the enactment of the ACA, please refer to this archived report.

[6] For more information, see CRS Report R40834, *The Market Structure of the Health Insurance Industry*, by D. Andrew Austin and Thomas L. Hungerford; David Cutler, *Market Failure in Small Group Health Insurance*, National Bureau of Economic Research (NBER), October 1994, http://www.nber.org/papers/w4879.

[7] Before health care reform, insurance companies often counteracted this adverse selection by denying coverage to risky individuals or offering them coverage at higher insurance premium costs. While this helped to address the negative effects of adverse selection for insurance companies, it also led to some individuals not having insurance even if they wanted it.

[8] Prior to the ACA, insurers practices in the individual market for health insurance, such as denial of coverage to high-risk applicants, reduced the effects of adverse selection on risk pools, but also lead to more individuals without insurance. For more information on the ACA's private health insurance market reforms, see CRS Report R43048, *Overview of Private Health Insurance Provisions in the Patient Protection and Affordable Care Act (ACA)*, by Annie L. Mach.

[9] Some say that public policy should not encourage employer-sponsored health coverage, as it may provide incentives for some workers to stay in less-productive jobs in order to retain their health benefits. Under this interpretation, a market failure in the health care market may be the result of a worker's inability to accurately price the benefits of pursuing more productive lines of work, known as *opportunity costs*.

[10] Employer health insurance also benefits from the exclusion of premium contributions by employers from wage income, which benefits taxpayers with income tax liability. Insurance benefits are also excluded from the payroll tax although there are future benefits that partially offset the cost of the payroll tax.

[11] Executive Office the President, Council of Economic Advisers, *The Economic Effects of Health Care Reform on Small Businesses and Their Employees*, July 25, 2009.

[12] Health care coverage data is available at the U.S. Census Bureau and Bureau of Labor Statistics, HI01- Health Insurance Coverage Status and Type of Coverage by Selected Characteristics, Current Population Survey, http://www.census.gov/hhes/www/cpstables/032012/health/h01_000.htm. For critical analysis of ESI prior to enactment of the ACA, see Thomas C. Buchmueller and Alan C. Monheit, *Employer-Sponsored Health Insurance and the Promise of Health Insurance Reform*, National Bureau of Economic Research (NBER), Working Paper 14839, April 2009, http://www.nber.org/papers/w14839.pdf. Note that the ACA contains provisions to help address some of the authors' criticisms (e.g., access to affordable ESI coverage among small businesses).

[13] Some have voiced concerned that the ACA's 3.8% Medicare tax increase for higher-income tax filers could affect small business owners. Because this provision is targeted toward

individuals exceeding a certain threshold based on their modified adjusted gross income, and not business income, it is omitted from analysis in this report. For a description and analysis of this provision, see CRS Report R41413, *The 3.8% Medicare Contribution Tax on Unearned Income, Including Real Estate Transactions*, by Mark P. Keightley; and Tax Policy Center, Table T10-0084, March 1, 2010, http://www.taxpolicycenter.org/numbers /displayatab.cfm?DocID=2679&topic2ID=60&topic3ID=73& DocTypeID=.

[14] See CRS Report R41159, *Potential Employer Penalties Under the Patient Protection and Affordable Care Act (ACA)*, by Julie M. Whittaker for a more detailed explanation of the employer penalty.

[15] In other words, even if a business is considered to be a "small business" by other means (e.g., eligible for assistance from the Small Business Administration), they can still be classified as a "large employer" for the purposes of the ACA's employer penalty.

[16] Part-time workers are converted to FTEs by dividing the sum of part-time hours worked in a month by 120. This part-time calculation is then added to the amount of full-time workers to arrive at a total FTE count. With regard to multiple franchises under a single owner, ACA follows the Internal Revenue Service (IRS) aggregation rules governing "controlled groups" (26 USC §414). If one individual or entity owns (or has a substantial ownership interest in) several franchises, all those franchises are essentially considered one entity. In this case, for purposes of the 50-FTE rule under the employer penalty, the employees in each of the franchises must be aggregated to determine the number of FTEs.

[17] IRS has provided a safe harbor for employers to use the employee's W-2 income for this calculation (since most employers do not readily have information on an employee's household income).

[18] See CRS Report R41158, *Summary of Small Business Health Insurance Tax Credit Under the Patient Protection and Affordable Care Act (ACA)*, by Manon Scales and Annie L. Mach, for a more detailed discussion of the small business credit and detailed calculations of the tax credit.

[19] Ibid., see Table 3 for calculations.

[20] Note that small employers are not required to obtain health insurance coverage for their employees through a SHOP exchange; ACA explicitly states that enrollment in exchanges is voluntary, and no individuals or small employers may be compelled to enroll in exchange coverage (§ 1312(d) of ACA).

[21] In general, exchanges will offer comprehensive coverage that meets the standards to be certified as "qualified health plans" (QHPs). For more information about QHPs and exchanges (including SHOP exchanges), see CRS Report R42663, *Health Insurance Exchanges Under the Patient Protection and Affordable Care Act (ACA)*, by Bernadette Fernandez and Annie L. Mach.

[22] 78 *Federal Register* 33233, June 4, 2013.

[23] In the long-run, the labor supply is relatively fixed (inelastic). With a fixed aggregate labor supply, total payments to labor are fixed at any point in time. The compensation a firm offers a worker is equal to their direct wages plus any fringe benefits (e.g., health care). Thus, firms will respond to any increase in the price of offering those fringe benefits by either reducing the value of the fringe benefits or the value of the wages.

[24] Firms in capital-intensive industries might have less ability to pass any additional costs onto their workers, though.

[25] For more discussion of projections on ACA's effects on health care costs, coverage rates, etc., see Jonathan Gruber, "The Impacts of the Affordable Care Act: How Reasonable are the Projections?" *National Tax Journal* (September 2011), pp. 893-908 and Casey B. Mulligan,

"Health Reform, the Reward to Work, and Massachusetts," *New York Times Economix Blog*, March 6, 2013, at http://economix.blogs.nytimes.com/2013/03/06/health-reform-the-reward-towork-and-massachusetts/.

[26] eHealth Inc. Small Business Owners Unaware of Exchanges and Misunderstand Mandates and Tax Obligations Under the Affordable Care Act, http://news.ehealthinsurance.com/_ir/68/20132/eHealth%20Spring%202013%20Small%20Bus%20Survey.pdf.

[27] For a table containing data analysis of all employer firms, see the Appendix. As discussed earlier in this report, the SUSB dataset does not include non-employers (i.e., self-employed individuals). These self-employed individuals are excluded from analysis in this report because they could be working part-time as a side job (and possibly covered under an employer-sponsored plan or a spouse's group plan) or working full-time (and not subject to the employer penalty). If self-employed individuals are included among the number of "total firms" in the United States, then the share of businesses potentially subject to the employer penalty would be smaller.

[28] Note that these health care offer rates are not the same as employee take-up rates. For simplicity, the analysis in this report assumes that employees take-up employer-sponsored coverage rather than seek individual coverage in health exchanges or choose to pay ACA's individual penalty rather than a regular health care premium. This latter assumption might not hold for some workers (e.g., younger, healthier workers).

[29] Kaiser Family Foundation (KFF), *Employer Health Benefits Annual Survey*, 2012, http://ehbs.kff.org/pdf/2012/ 8345.pdf. In the past, the share of employers that offer health insurance have been higher than the share of the workers that take-up their employer's plan. KFF's reported offer rates are used in this analysis instead of employee take-up rates because a number of decisions affect the latter statistic. For example, some employees may not take-up their employer's health plan because they can obtain cheaper or more comprehensive coverage through a spouse's or family plan, they cannot afford to or choose not to pay for their share of their insurance premiums, etc. It is uncertain how the full implementation of ACA in 2014 will affect these statistics. While some employees might be affected by the other ACA provisions that are set to begin in 2014 (e.g., the individual mandate, insurance premium subsidies for low-income workers in individual health exchanges), these effects will probably not have a major effect on the number of firms that could be subject to the employer penalty.

[30] The KFF survey does not report data for firms with 1-2 workers.

[31] This calculation is computed by multiplying the share of employer firms (as shown in Table 1) times the share of firms that don't offer health benefits to their employees (as indicated by the 2012 KFF Employer Survey data), and then summing these numbers for firms with 50-199 workers and 200+ workers to arrive at a total estimate. In numerical terms, this is: (0.029*0.06) + (0.008*0.02) = 0.0019, or approximately 0.2% of all employer firms.

[32] This calculation is computed by multiplying the cumulative share of employees by employer size (as shown in Table 1) times the health care offer rates for the respective firm size found (as shown in Table 2), and then summing these numbers for firms with 50-199 workers and 200+ workers to arrive at a total estimate. In numerical terms, this is: (0.135*0.04) + (0.584*0.02) = 0.0171.

[33] For example, see Linda J. Blumberg et al., *Implications of the Affordable Care Act for American Business*, The Urban Institute, October 2012, http://www.urban.org/UploadedPDF/412675-Implications-of-the-Affordable-Care-Actfor-American-Business.pdf.

[34] Letter from Douglas Elmendorf, Director of the Congressional Budget Office to Honorable Nancy Pelosi, Speaker of the U.S. House of Representatives, May 25, 2010,

http://www.cbo.gov/sites/default/files/cbofiles/ftpdocs/113xx/doc11379/amendreconprop.pdf.

[35] Treasury Inspector General for Tax Administration, Affordable Care Act: Efforts to Implement the Small Business Health Care Tax Credit Were Mostly Successful, but Some Improvements Are Needed, 2011-40-103, September 19, 2011, http://www.treasury.gov/tigta/auditreports/2011reports/201140103fr.pdf.

[36] U.S. Government Accountability Office, *Small Employer Health Tax Credit: Factors Contributing to Low Use and Complexity*, GAO-12-549, 2012, http://www.gao.gov/assets/600/590832.pdf. GAO's independent audit was lower than the U.S. Department of the Treasury's Inspector General for Tax Administration's 2011 claim that 228,000 small businesses applied for the health care credit.

[37] This estimate is based on GAO's methodology of data from the Medical Expenditure Panel Survey. See U.S. Government Accountability Office, *Small Employer Health Tax Credit: Factors Contributing to Low Use and Complexity*, GAO-12-549, 2012, p. 10, http://www.gao.gov/assets/600/590832.pdf.

[38] Ibid., p. 12.

[39] Ibid., p. 13. Some tax preparers said that it takes their clients from two to eight hours, or possibly longer, to gather the necessary information to calculate the credit and that the tax preparers spent, in general, three to five hours calculating the credit. If a small business tax accountant charges approximately $122 an hour, then a small business owner would likely need to project a tax credit of at least $350 to $600 just to cover the cost of hiring an accountant to calculate the credit—in addition to the cost of the time spent gathering any necessary information. GAO used this figure from a 2008 National Society of Accountants survey that estimated the hourly tax preparer fee to be $122 an hour.

[40] For more information on SHOP exchanges and current status of implementation, see CRS Report R42663, *Health Insurance Exchanges Under the Patient Protection and Affordable Care Act (ACA)*, by Bernadette Fernandez Annie L. Mach.

[41] Kaiser Family Foundation, *Employer Health Benefits Annual Survey*, 2012, http://ehbs.kff.org/pdf/2012/8345.pdf.

[42] These issues are discussed in Executive Office the President, Council of Economic Advisers, *The Economic Effects of Health Care Reform on Small Businesses and Their Employees*, July 25, 2009, http://www.whitehouse.gov/assets/ documents/CEA-smallbusiness-july24.pdf.

[43] Some of these concerns are summarized in Testimony of Larry Schuler on behalf of the National Restaurant Association, in U.S. Congress, House Committee on Energy and Commerce, Subcommittee on Health, Obamacare's Impact on Jobs, 112th Cong., 1st sess., March 30, 2011, http://www.restaurant.org/Downloads/PDFs/advocacy/ 20130313_hc_energycommerce_nra_testimony; and Testimony of Tom Boucher on behalf of the National Restaurant Association, in U.S. Congress, House Committee on Energy and Commerce, Subcommittee on Health, Obamacare's Impact on Jobs, 113th Cong., 1st sess., March 13, 2013, http://www.restaurant.org/Downloads/PDFs/advocacy/20130313_hc_energy commerce_nra_testimony.

[44] See comments of Mark Zandi indicating the predicted employment effects were lower than expected and appear to be modest in Danielle Kurtzleben, "Businesses Applaud Affordable Care Act," *U.S. News and World Report*, July 3, 2013, http://news.yahoo.com/businesses-applaud-affordable-care-act-delay-135819141.html;_ylt=A2KJ2UbEatRRW3oAENDQtDMD.

[45] Letter from Douglas Elmendorf, Director, Congressional Budget Office, to Honorable Paul Ryan, Chairman, House of Representatives Committee on the Budget, July 30, 2013, http://www.cbo.gov/sites/default/files/cbofiles/ attachments/44465-ACA.pdf.

[46] For example, see Ezra Klein, "Obamacare's employer mandate shouldn't be delayed. It should be repealed," *The Washington Post Wonkblog*, July 2, 2013, http://www.washingtonpost.com/blogs/wonkblog/wp/2013/07/02/ obamacares-employer-mandate-shouldnt-be-delayed-it-should-be-repealed/ and Tyler Cowan, "Repeal the employer mandate altogether," Marginal Revolution Blog, July 3, 2013, http://marginalrevolution.com/marginalrevolution /2013/ 07/repeal-the-employer-mandate-altogether.html.

[47] For example, see the Small Business Health Relief Act of 2013 (H.R. 1558, S. 24) and the American Job Protection Act (S. 399). None of these bills have been reported out of committee.

[48] Much of this logic is based on research pertaining to the use of coverage mandates in the health insurance market. For example, see Jonathan Gruber, *Covering the Uninsured in the U.S.*, National Bureau of Economic Research (NBER), Working Paper 13758, January 2008, http://www.nber.org/papers/w13758.pdf.

[49] Sen. Joe Donnelly and Sen. Susan Collins, "ObamaCare's Definition of Full-Time Job Needs Revising," *Wall Street Journal*, July 18, 2013, http://online.wsj.com/article/SB1000142 4127887323309404578611490682767344.html.

[50] For example, see Mark Peters and Douglas Belkin, "Health Law Pinches Colleges," *Wall Street Journal*, January 18, 2013, http://online.wsj.com/article/SB10001424 1278873 23635504578213502177768898.html.

[51] International Foundation of Employee Benefit Plans, *2013 Employer-Sponsored Health Care: ACA's Impact*, 2013, http://www.ifebp.org/pdf/research/2103ACAImpactSurvey.pdf. For more details on the survey methodology, see the report's introduction.

[52] Mercer, *Health Reform Poses Biggest Challenge to Companies with the Most Part-Time and Low Paid Employees*, August 8, 2012, http://www.mercer.us/press-releases/1472805. Details about the survey's methodology and summary statistics of the respondents are not included in this press release.

[53] For example, see Towers Watson, *Nearly Half of U.S. Employers Contemplating Changes to Reward Programs in Light of Health Care Reform*, June 13, 2013, http://www.towers watson.com/en/Press/2013/06/Nearly-Half-of-USEmployers-Contemplating-Changes-to-Reward-Programs-in-Light-of-Health-Care-Reform; and Challenger, Gray & Christmas, Inc., *Majority of Employers Plan to Maintain Health Coverage*, June 26, 2013, http://www.challengergray.com/press/PressRelease. aspx?PressUid=275.

[54] U.C. Berkeley Labor Center, *Data Brief: Which Workers are Most at Risk of Reduced Work Hours Under the Affordable Care Act?*, February 2013, http://laborcenter.berkeley.edu /healthcare/reduced_work_hours13.pdf.

[55] Helene Jorgensen and Dean Baker, *The Affordable Care Act: A Hidden Jobs Killer?*, Center for Economic and Policy Research, July 2013, http://www.cepr.net/documents /publications/aca-job-killer-2013-07.pdf.

[56] See Quantria Strategies LLC for the Small Business Administration's Office of Advocacy, *Health Insurance in the Small Business Market: Availability, Coverage and the Effect of Tax Incentives*, September 2011, p. 28, http://www.sba.gov/sites/default/files/386tot.pdf.

[57] For example, the median age for a worker in "food services and drinking places" was 28.8 in 2012 and 37.9 in "retail trade." This data does *not* control for firm size. See Bureau of Labor Statistics, "Labor Force Statistics from the Current Population Survey (2012)," http://www.bls.gov/cps/industry_age.htm.

58 See Testimony of Tom Boucher on behalf of the National Restaurant Association, in U.S. Congress, House Committee on Energy and Commerce, Subcommittee on Health, Obamacare's Impact on Jobs, 113th Cong., 1st sess., March 13, 2013, http://www.restaurant.org/Downloads/PDFs/advocacy/ 20130313_hc_energycommerce_nra_testimony.

59 Tom Gara, "Obamacare and Restaurants: Less Pain than Feared," *The Wall Street Journal,* Corporate Intelligence Blog, May 14, 2013, http://blogs.wsj.com/corporate-intelligence /2013/05/14/obamacare-and-restaurants-less-pain-thanfeared/.

60 See CRS Report R41997, *Definition of Income for Certain Medicaid Provisions and Premium Credits in ACA*, coordinated by Christine Scott; and CRS Report R41210, *Medicaid and the State Children's Health Insurance Program (CHIP) Provisions in ACA: Summary and Timeline*, by Evelyne P. Baumrucker et al.

61 In its 2012 decision in *National Federation of Independent Business v. Sebelius*, the Supreme Court held that the federal government cannot terminate current Medicaid program federal matching funds if a state refuses to expand its Medicaid program. If a state accepts the new ACA Medicaid expansion funds, it must abide by the new expansion coverage rules, but, based on the Court's opinion, it appears that a state can refuse to participate in the expansion without losing any of its current federal Medicaid matching funds. See CRS Report R41664, *ACA: A Brief Overview of the Law, Implementation, and Legal Challenges*, coordinated by Charles S. Redhead.

62 For the latest status of states' decisions to participate in the ACA Medicaid expansion, see Kaiser Family Foundation, *Status of State Action on the Medicaid Expansion Decision*, http://kff.org/medicaid/state-indicator/state-activityaround-expanding-medicaid-under-the-affordable-care-act/.

63 See Testimony of Diana Furchtgott-Roth, Senior Fellow at the Manhattan Institute, U.S. Congress, House Committee on Energy and Commerce, Subcommittee on Health, *Obamacare's Impact on Jobs*, 113th Cong., 1st sess., March 13, 2013, http://docs.house.gov/meetings/IF/IF14/20130313/100443/HMTG-113-IF14-Wstate-Furchtgott-RothD-20130313.pdf.

64 For example, see Avik Roy, "Employers Can Minimize Their Exposure To Obamacare's Penalties By Offering Low-Cost 'Skinny' Coverage," *Forbes (Online)*, May 21, 2013, http://www.forbes.com/sites/theapothecary/2013/05/21/ employers-can-minimize-their-exposure-to-obamacares-health-insurance-mandate-by-offering-low-cost-skinnycoverage/.

65 See Testimony of Linda Blumberg, Senior Fellow at the Urban Institute, U.S. Congress, House Committee on Energy and Commerce, Subcommittee on Health, *Obamacare's Impact on Jobs*, 113th Cong., 1st sess., March 13, 2013, http://docs.house.gov/meetings/IF /IF14/20130313/ 100443/HMTG-113-IF14-Wstate-BlumbergL-20130313.pdf.

66 This was computed assuming $11.50 an hour for someone working 40 hours per week (totaling $23,920 a year).

67 A few examples can be used to support this point, using the $2 million payroll exclusion cap. A firm paying all of its workers the a salary of $44,128 (the average worker salary across all firm sizes and industries, as shown in Table 4) would not be affected by the cap because they would not exceed the 50-FTE employee threshold (because they could hire up to 45 employees under the $2 million cap); a firm paying all of its workers a salary of $39,300 (the average worker salary in firms with 45-50 employees) would also not be affected by the cap because they would not exceed the 50-FTE employee threshold (because they could hire up to 50 employees under the $2 million cap); and a firm paying all of its workers a salary of $39,458 (the average worker salary in firms with 50-74 employees) would also not

be affected by the cap because they would not exceed the 50-FTE employee threshold (because they could hire up to 50 employees under the $2 million cap).

[68] Determinations whether a firm was eligible under the $2 million payroll cap were based on average payroll calculations per firm within an industry. The $2 million cap is simply an illustration.

[69] This is calculated by: (the minimum wage of $7.25)*(40 hours per week)*(52 weeks in a year) = $15,080. Note that this definition of a "full-time" worker is 40 hours per week, whereas the statutory definition in ACA is 30 hours per week.

[70] For example, the Census Bureau's Statistics of U.S. Business Annual Data can be used to calculate analysis similar to Table 4, by North American Industry Classification System (NAICS) code.

[71] 26 U.S.C. 199. See U.S. Congress, Senate Committee on the Budget, *Tax Expenditures: Compendium of Background Material on Individual Provisions*, committee print, prepared by the Congressional Research Service, 112th Cong., 2nd sess., December 2012, S. Prt. 112-45 (Washington: GPO, 2012), pp. 509-512.

[72] NAICS classifications are one test that a tax filer can use, in part, to claim a Section 199 production activities tax deduction.

[73] Department of the Treasury, *General Explanations of the Administration's Fiscal Year 2014 Revenue Proposals*, April 2013, p.30, http://www.treasury.gov/resource-center/tax-policy/Documents/General-Explanations-FY2014.pdf.

[74] Ibid., p. 242.

INDEX

A

access, vii, viii, ix, x, 2, 3, 4, 5, 7, 8, 14, 24, 27, 28, 37, 40, 46, 56, 58, 59, 75, 77, 78, 95, 107
accommodation, 105
accounting, xii, 30, 84, 94, 96
adjustment, 20, 21, 22, 79, 89
administrators, 21
adolescents, 60
adults, 78, 85
advocacy, 64, 110, 112
age, viii, xi, 2, 5, 6, 8, 9, 16, 26, 28, 39, 40, 45, 46, 54, 61, 63, 66, 67, 68, 78, 79, 80, 85, 88, 99, 111
agencies, 54
aggregation, 108
Alaska, 100
annual review, 57
Appropriations Act, 33
assessment, 21
assets, 110
audit, 110
authority, 6, 7, 11, 13, 28, 57

B

background information, xi, 54
barriers, xii, 84
blogs, 109, 111, 112
Bureau of Labor Statistics, 99, 107, 111
businesses, xi, xii, 83, 84, 85, 87, 88, 90, 93, 94, 95, 96, 100, 101, 104, 106, 107, 109, 110

C

cancer, 68
CDC, 60, 78
Census, 31, 92, 93, 102, 106, 107, 113
certification, 10, 15, 68
CFR, 79
charities, 90
childhood, 87
children, xi, 8, 9, 45, 46, 54, 57, 60, 61, 62, 63, 76, 78, 80
citizens, 14, 29, 34
clients, 110
clinical trials, 10, 68
community, 68, 88, 92
compensation, 5, 108
compensation package, 5
compliance, xii, 11, 55, 83, 85, 91, 96, 97, 99, 104
complications, 103
composition, viii, 2
computation, 100
conflict, 56
Congress, 1, 7, 19, 26, 34, 37, 79, 97, 105, 110, 112, 113

Congressional Budget Office, 13, 32, 94, 109, 111
Consolidated Appropriations Act, 33
consulting, 98
consumer protection, viii, 2, 7, 27, 46, 55, 56, 63
consumers, xi, 27, 51, 53, 57, 80
coordination, 33, 34, 66
costs of compliance, 100
covering, vii, 1, 6, 21, 32, 39, 76, 77, 79
critical analysis, 107
CT, 32
customers, 103

D

data analysis, 109
deficit, 27
demographic characteristics, 5, 6, 7
denial, 63, 79, 107
Department of Defense, 33
Department of Health and Human Services, 17, 34, 35, 57, 78, 85
Department of the Treasury, 113
depth, ix, 3, 89
diabetes, 6, 66
direct cost(s), 85
disability, 35, 45, 67
disbursement, 19
disclosure, 55, 80
discrimination, viii, xi, 2, 54, 57
diseases, 78, 86
disorder, 32, 51
distortions, 97
District of Columbia, 29, 80, 100
domestic violence, 35, 67
dosing, 78

E

economic status, 28
economic theory, 87
elective abortion, 30, 35
eligibility criteria, 8, 33, 34, 44, 62
emergency, 9, 32, 51, 63, 64
empirical studies, 106
employee compensation, 25
employees, viii, ix, x, xii, 2, 3, 4, 5, 6, 8, 12, 24, 25, 27, 31, 32, 34, 43, 44, 51, 55, 59, 62, 76, 77, 79, 84, 85, 87, 88, 89, 90, 91, 92, 93, 94, 95, 96, 97, 98, 99, 100, 101, 102, 103, 104, 105, 106, 108, 109, 112
employers, vii, viii, ix, x, xii, 1, 2, 3, 4, 5, 6, 7, 12, 24, 25, 27, 28, 32, 37, 38, 43, 44, 46, 51, 55, 70, 77, 79, 84, 85, 88, 89, 90, 91, 92, 94, 95, 96, 97, 98, 100, 101, 107, 108, 109, 112
employment, 5, 34, 55, 62, 76, 77, 87, 93, 96, 106, 110
employment status, 5
endangered, 35
energy, 110
enforcement, 56, 77, 85
enrollee, viii, 2, 12, 18, 21, 30, 32, 60, 63, 64, 65, 67
enrollment, 8, 12, 16, 21, 29, 39, 44, 59, 63, 64, 67, 68, 72, 80, 108
ESI, 4, 14, 87, 88, 92, 107
essential health benefits, viii, 2, 9, 10, 12, 15, 17, 38, 39, 46, 51, 58
evidence, 35, 60, 61, 63, 66, 67
exclusion, 63, 96, 102, 107, 112
exposure, 104, 112
externalities, 86, 87

F

faith, 58
families, 4, 12, 38, 51, 55, 95, 99
family members, 8, 25
FDA, 79
federal agency, 78
federal funds, 29, 30, 33, 35
federal government, 7, 11, 13, 15, 17, 18, 26, 29, 33, 55, 92, 112
Federal Government, 32
federal law, 7, 31, 60, 61, 63, 67, 79
Federal Register, 32, 69, 70, 71, 72, 73, 74, 78, 79, 80, 81, 100, 108
federal regulations, 73

federalism, 55
financial, vii, viii, x, 1, 2, 4, 6, 13, 18, 24, 26, 30, 31, 33, 45, 51, 78
financial incentives, x, 4, 24, 30
financial support, 78
firm size, 91, 94, 109, 111, 112
flaws, 86
flexibility, 26
food, 99, 101, 105, 111
food services, 111
formula, 21, 104
fraud, 8, 60
fringe benefits, 108
funding, 13, 17, 22, 28, 30, 33
funds, 19, 22, 23, 26, 30, 32, 33, 34, 35, 76, 77, 112

G

GAO, xii, 80, 84, 95, 110
genetic information, 35, 67
geography, 81
government intervention, 86
grants, 13
growth, 34, 91, 106
guidance, 17, 34, 46, 78
guidelines, 60, 61, 78, 79, 100

H

Hawaii, 100
Health and Human Services, xi, 44, 51, 54, 58, 77, 78, 79
health care, x, xi, xii, 4, 6, 9, 10, 18, 19, 24, 27, 30, 31, 33, 35, 54, 63, 64, 65, 66, 67, 68, 78, 80, 83, 84, 85, 86, 87, 91, 94, 95, 98, 99, 103, 104, 107, 108, 109, 110
health care costs, 108
health care professionals, 9, 63, 64
health condition, xi, 10, 23, 29, 54, 57, 63, 66, 67
health information, 66
health insurance coverage, vii, viii, ix, x, xii, 1, 2, 3, 4, 6, 12, 16, 23, 24, 26, 28, 38, 42, 45, 51, 64, 69, 71, 72, 73, 77, 80, 83, 89, 91, 94, 95, 96, 99, 101, 106, 108
health insurance exchanges, vii, x, xii, 32, 37, 38, 83, 84
health insurance market, vii, ix, x, xi, 1, 3, 4, 5, 20, 31, 32, 37, 38, 45, 51, 53, 54, 55, 76, 86, 107, 111
health plans, vii, viii, x, xi, 1, 2, 9, 10, 11, 13, 19, 20, 21, 30, 32, 35, 37, 38, 45, 46, 51, 53, 54, 55, 56, 58, 60, 62, 63, 66, 67, 68, 69, 70, 71, 72, 73, 75, 76, 77, 79, 91, 103, 108
health problems, viii, 2, 88
health promotion, 66
health services, xi, 9, 11, 20, 54, 57, 60, 70
health status, viii, ix, xi, 2, 4, 5, 6, 7, 10, 20, 23, 35, 54, 66, 67, 86, 87
heart disease, 66
HHS, 8, 9, 11, 13, 16, 19, 21, 23, 26, 27, 28, 29, 30, 31, 32, 33, 34, 35, 57, 59, 62, 63, 64, 69, 70, 71, 72, 73, 78, 79, 80, 85, 91, 100
hiring, 85, 91, 96, 97, 103, 104, 110
history, viii, 2
HIV, 78
HIV/AIDS, 78
hospitalization, 32, 51, 66
House, 80, 109, 110, 111, 112
House of Representatives, 109, 111
household income, ix, 3, 14, 23, 24, 26, 33, 34, 89, 99, 100, 101, 108

I

ID, 32
immigrants, 33
immunization, 78
improvements, 98
income, ix, 3, 14, 18, 23, 26, 33, 34, 44, 85, 90, 92, 94, 96, 99, 100, 101, 103, 107, 108, 109
income tax, ix, 3, 14, 18, 23, 90, 107
Indians, 33
industries, 97, 99, 101, 102, 103, 105, 108, 112

industry, 51, 98, 99, 101, 102, 103, 111, 113
infants, 60
infertility, 7
inflation, 23, 100
insurance policy, 32, 64
intelligence, 112
Internal Revenue Service, 23, 95, 108
intervention, 66
issues, vii, 6, 33, 55, 77, 78, 85, 87, 91, 96, 110

J

job creation, 106
justification, 8, 57, 86

L

labor market, 97, 98
laws, 6, 7, 19, 27, 30
laws and regulations, 7, 27
lead, 20, 86, 92, 99, 107
leadership, 78
legislation, 97
lifetime, xi, 9, 53, 57, 58, 59
light, 99
liquidity, 99
loans, 17, 19, 33, 40

M

majority, 42, 93, 94
management, 19, 32, 51, 66
market failure, 86, 107
market segment, xi, 5, 6, 54, 56, 67
market structure, ix, 3
marketing, 13, 15, 44, 55
measurement, 98
media, 100
median, 99, 111
Medicaid, viii, 3, 4, 15, 16, 19, 23, 26, 32, 33, 34, 57, 58, 85, 99, 100, 112
medical, x, xi, 6, 9, 11, 12, 20, 24, 31, 32, 35, 38, 42, 44, 46, 54, 57, 58, 60, 62, 63, 65, 66, 67, 68, 76, 77
medical history, 6, 20, 35, 67
Medicare, viii, 3, 4, 15, 23, 28, 33, 34, 57, 87, 107
medicine, 66
mental health, 32, 51
mental illness, 35, 67
methodology, 110, 111
minimum wage, 92, 101, 113
misunderstanding, 92
modifications, 64, 101

N

negative effects, 107
negative externality, 86
North America, 103, 113
nutrition, 66

O

Obama, xii, 83, 85, 88, 96, 104
Obama Administration, 85, 88, 104
Obama, President, xii, 84, 104
officials, 54
old age, 87
operations, 33
opportunities, 5
opportunity costs, 107
ownership, 80, 93, 106, 108

P

pain, 112
parity, 7
participants, xi, 54, 66, 72
Patient Protection and Affordable Care Act, v, vii, ix, x, xi, 1, 3, 10, 16, 32, 33, 35, 37, 44, 45, 49, 51, 53, 54, 77, 79, 80, 83, 84, 107, 108, 110
payroll, 90, 92, 93, 98, 101, 102, 103, 104, 106, 107, 112, 113

penalties, vii, ix, 1, 3, 24, 27, 66, 92, 101, 102
permit, 30, 64
PHI, vii, viii, ix, 1, 2, 3
physical fitness, 66
platinum, 11, 16, 39, 44
policy, 69, 70, 71, 72, 73, 75, 96, 102, 113
pools, x, 4, 20, 24, 29, 34, 58, 87, 88, 92, 107
population, 4, 11, 12, 21, 44, 78
poverty, 14, 85, 100
pre-existing condition, viii, ix, 2, 3, 6, 9, 20, 29, 31, 87, 88
pregnancy, 35
prescription drugs, 32, 51
preservation, 30
President, xii, 84, 104, 107, 110
President Obama, xii, 84, 104
prevention, 66, 78
private firms, 5
profit, 19, 21, 25, 98
project, 110
protection, 30
Public Health Service Act, 31, 77
public policy, 107

R

rape, 35
recommendations, 78
recovery, 98
reform(s), viii, x, xi, 2, 4, 46, 54, 55, 56, 67, 69, 70, 71, 72, 73, 75, 79, 107, 109, 110, 111
regulations, xi, 9, 10, 11, 15, 16, 22, 27, 32, 54, 56, 59, 65, 70, 78, 80
reinsurance, 20, 21, 22, 28, 31
requirements, vii, viii, ix, x, xi, 1, 2, 3, 7, 9, 11, 15, 16, 18, 19, 24, 26, 27, 29, 30, 31, 37, 38, 39, 40, 42, 43, 44, 45, 46, 52, 53, 54, 55, 56, 57, 58, 60, 61, 62, 63, 65, 68, 71, 72, 73, 77, 79, 80
researchers, 98
reserves, 33
resources, 32, 33, 34, 78, 79, 80, 86
response, 11, 97
restaurants, 103, 112
restrictions, xi, 10, 23, 54, 60, 66
retail, 99, 111
revenue, 9, 62, 96, 103, 104, 105
rewards, 67
rights, 80
risk, xii, 6, 20, 21, 22, 24, 29, 31, 32, 33, 34, 42, 58, 66, 76, 77, 84, 86, 87, 88, 96, 107
risk assessment, 66
risk profile, 6, 88, 96
rules, ix, xii, 3, 7, 11, 27, 55, 62, 68, 73, 77, 81, 84, 108, 112

S

safety, 66
savings, 32
savings account, 32
scope, 7, 10, 46, 55, 56, 68, 88, 100
self-employed, 76, 109
Senate, 26, 34, 79, 80, 113
services, x, 4, 6, 11, 16, 18, 20, 24, 29, 30, 31, 32, 35, 51, 54, 59, 60, 61, 63, 64, 66, 70, 78, 79
silver, 11, 15, 16, 18, 19, 20, 39
simulations, 94
small businesses, ix, xi, xii, 4, 12, 38, 40, 83, 84, 85, 86, 88, 91, 92, 95, 99, 104, 106, 107, 110
small firms, 87, 94, 95
smoking, 66
smoking cessation, 66
society, 86, 87
spending, 27
spillover effects, 86, 87
stakeholders, 65
state laws, 7, 30
statistics, 109, 111
storage, 80
stress, 66
structure, vii, ix, x, 2, 3, 4, 55
Subsidies, 18, 32
subsidy, 18, 30, 33, 99
substance use, 32, 51

substitutes, 38
Supreme Court, 85, 112
suspensions, 35

T

target, 21, 101, 103
Task Force, 60, 78
tax credits, viii, 2, 13, 14, 18, 20, 26, 34, 39, 40, 41, 42, 43, 44, 51
tax deduction, 103, 113
tax increase, 107
taxes, 62, 90
taxpayers, 95, 107
techniques, 61
technology, 66
territory, 78
tobacco, 68, 81
trade, 76, 111
trade union, 76
Treasury, 27, 31, 33, 34, 58, 64, 69, 70, 71, 72, 73, 79, 80, 105, 110
Treasury Secretary, 33, 34
treatment, 32, 51, 61, 63, 68, 103
trial, xi, 54, 66, 67, 68

U

U.S. Department of the Treasury, 110
uniform, ix, xi, 3, 25, 54, 56, 57, 64, 65, 80, 104
uninsured, 29, 78, 87, 103
unions, 43
United, vii, 1, 4, 5, 14, 23, 34, 60, 79, 109
United States, vii, 1, 4, 5, 14, 23, 34, 60, 79, 109
urban, 109
Urban Institute, 109, 112

V

vaccine, 78
variations, 87
vision, 32, 45, 51

W

wages, 25, 34, 87, 90, 92, 99, 100, 101, 105, 108
waiver, 26, 27, 78
Washington, 26, 34, 111, 113
wealth, 86
web, 65, 66
weight management, 66
welfare, 92
wellness, 19, 30, 31, 32, 51, 66, 67, 80
White House, 107
workers, xii, 5, 25, 45, 55, 76, 84, 85, 86, 88, 89, 92, 93, 94, 95, 96, 97, 98, 99, 100, 101, 102, 103, 104, 107, 108, 109, 112
workforce, 85, 98
working population, 87